Song of the Prophets

Song *of*
the Prophets

The Unity of Religious Ideals

Hazrat Inayat Khan

OMEGA PUBLICATIONS, INC.

New Lebanon, New York

©2009 Omega Publications

Manufactured in the United States of America.
Printed and bound by Sheridan Books, Inc., Ann Arbor, Michigan.

Printed on acid-free paper with sewn and glued binding.
Cover design by Yasodhara Lillydahl.
Editorial and production services by Green Lion Press.

Cataloguing-in-Publication Data
ISBN 0-930872-80-0
ISBN-13 is 978-0930872-90-9

1. Inayat Khan, works. 2. Religion. 3. Sufism. 4. Spirituality.

Library of Congress Control Number: 2009924391

10 9 8 7 6 5 4 3 2 1

Contents

Editor's Note to the 2009 Edition

The Song of the Prophets:The Unity of Religious Ideals is a new and improved edition of Sufi Order Publications' long out of print volume *The Unity of Religious Ideals.* In addition to the revised title and new cover design, corrections have been made to prior textual errors. Readers will be pleased to find that *Song of the Prophets* is a well-designed quality edition, with a sewn binding made to last through years of dedicated use.

Editor's Note to the 1979 Edition

The first volume entitled *The Unity of Religious Ideals* was published in London in 1927 shortly after Hazrat Inayat Khan died. It was edited mainly from a series of papers known as the Religious Gathekas, which are transcripts of the sermons given by Hazrat Inayat Khan at Universal Worship services between 1924 and 1926. Additional material was included on various prophets from the different traditions and on the Sufi Order.

For the Sufi Message volumes, the original book was re-edited and considerably altered; this version appeared in 1963.

For the 1979 edition, we have returned to the original transcripts and have attempted to present the teachings in the very words which Hazrat Inayat Khan spoke, as far as possible. This volume now contains almost all of the material from the sermons, as well as the material on the various teachers of mankind. Because this has considerably expanded the book, material concerning the Sufi Order and the Universal Worship has been reserved for a future volume.

Professor Donald A. Graham

Introduction
by Pir Vilayat Inayat Khan

In these pages, Hazrat Inayat Khan unmasks the mystery of perhaps the most vexing question ever to challenge the human mind, running across the tides of religious growth throughout history. What exactly is it that one means by God?

Undoubtedly man's intuition of being an integral part of a greater whole (first dimly felt, then ritualized), apart from filling him with an awe that sometimes contributed towards curbing his ego, averred itself to be the driving force of human evolution by luring him beyond his immediate environment and the reach of his consciousness into vaster horizons of understanding. But it was only when this same intuition led him to envision God as a perfect model that man really discovered his purpose in the universe: to manifest the divine perfection he inherits. Hazrat Inayat Khan shows how efforts to make the intuition of God intelligible by a concept of God can only prove to be limiting. Consequently, the arbitrary concepts of God by well-meaning, most often pious people have alienated many from attaching credence to their direct intuition of God. Mysticism is "rising to the pitch where one feels God," which Hazrat Inayat Khan calls "making God a reality instead of an imagination." There comes a time when one sees that this is all one being.

Of course, Hazrat Inayat Khan voices the awakening planetary awareness of the underlying unity behind the variety of religious forms and loyalties. Yet he does not advocate "tuning all the keys of the piano to the same note." But there can be no doubt that the most imperious need of the human being, though often quashed into oblivion, is to be inspired and hoisted beyond himself in a supreme act of glorification where he gives vent to his hunch of a cosmic celebration in the heavens crowning the drama on the earth: the only thing that makes ultimate sense of life. Such a festival could not but include all religious faiths. Hazrat Inayat Khan called it the Universal Worship, the Church of All and of all religions: the very expression of the Message in our time. When he was inspired to found it he said: "That which the prophets of the past could not bring about, owing to the difficult conditions in their time, is brought about today as the fulfillment of their prayers offered for thousands of years."

Pir Vilayat Inayat Khan

Religion

Religion

Perhaps a person belongs to the best religion in the world. He does not live it, but belongs to it. He says that he is a Muslim, or a Christian, or a Jew. He is sure it is the best religion, but at the same time he does not care to live it—he just belongs to it, and thinks that belonging to a certain religion, which is an accepted religion, is all that is needed. And people of all different religions have made it appear so, owing to their enthusiasm, and forced by their mission in life. For they have made facilities for those who belong to their particular religion, saying that by the very fact of their belonging to that particular religion they will be saved on the Day of Judgment, while others, with all their good actions, will not be saved, because they do not belong to that particular religion. This is a man-made idea, not God-made. God is not the Father of one sect; God is the Father of the whole world, and all are entitled to be called His children, whether worthy or unworthy. And in fact it is man's attitude toward God and Truth which can bring him closer to God, Who is the ideal of every soul. And if this attitude is not developed, then, whatever a man's religion be, he has failed to live it. Therefore, what is important in life is to try and live the religion to which one belongs, or that one esteems, or that one believes to be one's religion.

But one must always know that religion has a body and has a soul. Whatever body of religion you may touch, you touch the soul; but if you touch the soul, you touch all its bodies, which are like its organs. And all the organs constitute one body, which is the body of *the* religion, the religion (which is the religion of Alpha and Omega) which was and which is and which will always be. Therefore the dispute, "I am right and you are wrong," in the path of religion is not necessary. We do not know what is in the heart of man. If outwardly he seems to be a Jew, a Christian, a Muslim, or a Buddhist, we are not the judge of his religion, for every soul has a religion peculiar to itself, and no one else is entitled to judge its religion. There may be a person in a very humble garb, without any appearance of belief in God, or of piety or orthodoxy, and he may have a religion hidden in his heart which not everybody can understand. And there may be a person who is highly evolved, and his outward conduct, which alone manifests to people's views, may appear to be altogether contrary to their own way of looking at things, and they may accuse him of being a materialist or an unbeliever, or someone who is far from God and Truth. And yet we do not know; sometimes appearances are merely illusions; behind them there may be the deepest religious devotion or the highest ideal hidden, of which we know very little.

For the Sufi, therefore, the best thing is to respect man's belief, whatever it may be, his ideal, whatever it may be, his way of looking at life, even if it be quite different from one's own way of looking at it. It is this spirit of tolerance that, when developed, will bring about the brotherhood which is the essence of religion and the want of the day.

The idea that you are different and I am different; your religion is different and my religion is different; your belief is different and my belief is different—that will not unite, that will only divide humanity. Those who, with the excuse of their great faith in their own religion, hurt the feeling of another and divide humanity, (whose Source and Goal is the same) abuse religion, whatever be their faith. The Message, (whenever) at whatever period it came to the world, did not come to a certain section of humanity; it did not come to raise only some few people who perhaps accepted the faith, the Message, or a particular organized Church. No, all these things came afterwards. The rain does not fall in a certain land only; the sun does not shine upon a certain country only. All that is from God is for all souls. If they are worthy, they deserve it; it is their reward; if they are unworthy, they are the more entitled to it. Verily, blessing is for every soul; for every soul, whatever be his faith or belief, belongs to God.

In the ancient Sanskrit language the word for religion is *Dharma*, which means duty. Now, there are two things in the world, one of which we may describe as free choice of action and the other as duty. Everybody follows either the way of free choice or the way of duty. As an example we may think of the child who sees the fire, and wants to touch it, and does so. This action will show a certain disagreeable result which teaches the child a certain thing. This teaching might also have come to the child as a warning from the parents, telling the child that the result of the action would be burning. The child might thus refrain from doing a certain action for the reason that it accepted the warning of the parents before burning its hand.

Every child is born in life a pupil, one who is willing to learn and willing to believe. As the Prophet Muhammad says: "Every soul is born on earth a believer; it is only afterwards that he turns into an unbeliever." It is certain that if one had not been born a believer one would never have learned the language of one's country, because if anyone had tried to teach the words and one had refused to accept the teachings as true, one would never have learned the names and character of things. For instance, if it were said, "This is water," and one had not believed it, and had thought, "It is fruit," then one would never really have known what was water and what fruit. A child is born with the tendency to believe and learn what it is taught.

The divine life has a certain capability to give life, and it gives this life as teaching to the children of earth, and this teaching is called *Dharma*, religion. Religions are many and different from one another, but only in form. Water is one and the same element, and formless, only it takes the shape of the channel which holds it and which it uses for its accommodation; and so the name water is changed into river, lake, sea, stream, pond, etc. So it is with religion; the essential truth is one, but the aspects are different. Those who fight about external forms will always fight; those who recognize the inner truth will not disagree, and thus will be able to harmonize the people of all religions.

Dharma has been given from time to time to the world, at times quietly, and sometimes with a loud voice; but it is a continual outpouring of the inner knowledge, of life, and of divine blessing. Those who stick to their old forms, closing their eyes to the inner truth, paralyze their Dharma by holding onto an old form while refusing the present stream that is sent. As life is the cause of activity, so such persons lose their activity; they remain where they are and are as dead. And when man has been thus paralyzed and shut out from further spiritual progress, he clings to outer forms which are not progressing. There was a time when the message was given while the people were wanting a messenger to come. During the time of Jesus Christ there were thousands and millions waiting for a messenger to come from above. The Master came, and did his service, and went away. Some realized then, and some are still waiting. But the One Who claimed to be Alpha and Omega is never absent; sometimes he appears on the surface, sometimes he is reserving himself.

When directed by the new spiritual inspiration, law, morals, education, and all departments of life come to new life; but if the spiritual current is lacking, then there is no further progress in the forms of life. People mostly think that the spiritual message must be something concrete and definite in the way of doctrines or principles; but that is a human tendency and does not belong to the divine nature, which is unlimited and life itself. The divine message is the answer to the cry of souls, individually and collectively; the divine message is life, and it is light. The sun does not teach anything, but in its light we learn to know all things. The sun does not cultivate the ground nor does it sow seed, but it helps the plant to grow, to flower, and to bear fruit.

The Sufi Message, in its utter infancy, strikes the note of the day, and promises the fulfillment of that purpose for which, now and then, the blessing from above descends, for spreading love and peace on earth and among men.

The Religion of the Heart

If anybody asks you, "What is Sufism? What religion is it?" you may answer, "Sufism is the religion of the heart, the religion in which one thing is most important, and that is to seek God in the heart of mankind."

There are three ways of seeking God in the human heart. The first way is to recognize the divine in every person and to be careful of every person with whom we come in contact, in our thought, speech, and action. Human personality is very delicate. The more living the heart, the more sensitive it is. But that which causes sensitiveness is the love-element in the heart, and love is God. The person whose heart is not sensitive is without feeling; his heart is not living, it is dead. In that case the Divine Spirit is buried in his heart. A person who is always concerned with his own feelings is so absorbed in himself that he has no time to think of another. His whole attention is taken up with his own feelings. He pities himself; he worries about his own pain, and is never open to sympathize with others. He who takes notice of the feeling of another person with whom he comes in contact, practices the first essential moral of Sufism.

The next way of practicing this religion is to think of the feeling of the person who is not at the moment before us. One feels for a person who is present, but one often neglects to feel for someone who is out of sight. One speaks well of someone to his face, but if one speaks well of someone when he is absent, that is greater. One sympathizes with the trouble of someone who is before one at the moment, but it is greater to sympathize with one who is far away. And the third way of realizing the Sufi principle is to recognize in one's own feeling the feeling of God; to realize every impulse of love that rises in one's heart as a direction from God; realizing that love is a divine spark in one's heart, to blow that spark until a flame may rise to illuminate the path of one's life.

The symbol of the Sufi Movement, which is a heart with wings, is symbolical of its ideal. The heart is both earthly and heavenly. The heart is a receptacle on earth of the Divine Spirit, and when it holds the Divine Spirit, it soars heavenward; the wings picture its rising. The crescent in the heart symbolizes responsiveness. It is the heart which responds to the spirit of God that rises. The crescent is a symbol of responsiveness because it grows fuller as the moon grows fuller by responding more and more to the sun as it progresses. The light one sees in the crescent is the light of the sun. As it gets more light with its increasing response, so it becomes fuller of the light of the sun. The star in the heart of the crescent represents the divine spark which is reflected in the human heart as love, and which helps the crescent toward its fullness.

The Sufi Message is the message of the day. It does not bring theories or doctrines to add to those existing already, which puzzle the human mind. What the world needs today is the message of love, harmony, and beauty, the absence of which is the only tragedy of life. The Sufi Message does not give a new law; it wakens in humanity the spirit of brotherhood, with tolerance on the part of each for the religion of the other, with forgiveness from each for the fault of the other. It teaches thoughtfulness and consideration, so as to create and maintain harmony in life; it teaches service and usefulness, which alone can make life in the world fruitful, in which lies the satisfaction of every soul.

～

When we think of the different religions which are known to humanity, we shall find that each of them brought to the world the message of love in some form or other. And now the question arises, who brought religion in the world? And the answer is that religion has always existed in the heart of man. Religion is the outcome of the heart, and among all races, however primitive, a certain religion has existed, perhaps incomprehensible to people more evolved in different directions. For religion is instinctive, and as it is instinctive, not only in the world of man but also in the lower creation one sees a glimpse of religious tendency. For instance, one finds among pet animals, such as the dog, the cat, or the horse, some such faithful creatures, and sometimes one has such experiences with them that one cannot today expect from mankind.

Besides this, the absorption that one sees among the birds, the little sparrows in the morning absorbed in the beauty of nature, so to speak, singing a song, a hymn to God: that all is religion, if we can understand it. For man has made his religion so narrow that he is not able to appreciate the broad religion of nature. By being narrow he has named his creed a religion, or the particular place of worship religion, or the book religion, or the form of service religion. If one would only think it is religion when one goes in the woods, in the forests, and stands alone in the forest near the silent trees standing in contemplation through the summer and winter, through all seasons! That silent contemplation, what does it give one, what thought arises? It lifts one up and makes one think that there is a religion.

One may call it a legend or a superstition or a story, but still there are experiences; we have the experience in India with the cobras: they never bite unless someone hurts them. The affection and the attachment that the doves show to their mates is something to learn and to understand. And there are many instances, many experiences of thoughtfulness, of consideration, and of the nature of attachment that one sees in the lower creation, and that make one think that there is an instinctive religion. Then there are stories known in the East about the elephants. In the herd of elephants there is one who always leads them and he has a stem of a tree in his trunk, and he goes on feeling the earth to see if there is a pit, or if it is a good way for the elephants to pass. And if there was a pit, he gives a warning to his followers, that they may not fall victims to this. When we consider the birds we see that there is among them a leader who knows and understands the coming and the continuing of rain and storm, and according to that he guides them, and they all follow him. By what is it all accounted for, this taking care of those who depend upon one, and then yielding, responding, trusting someone who guides one; it is not only in the human beings, but even more in the animals. And man, who is always supposed to have a religion and thinks that he has a religion, has always opposed in all ages the ones who have served him, those who have wished to awaken him from his errors. The saints and the sages and the great souls who have continually tried to work for him, they have always had to suffer and they were the ones who found opposition from all directions. And in this way man has shown a lesser tendency to religion than the animals.

But now, coming to understand what is the religion of the heart: It is said by the Sufis, "*Ishq Allah, Ma'abud Allah*," the same that one reads in the Bible, that "God is love." And if God is love, where is He to be found? Is He to be found in the seventh heaven or is He to be found in the heart of man? If He were so far away as to be in the seventh heaven then it would be most unfortunate for man to be kept far away from the very life and the very reason of his being. And it is toward this realization—that God is in the heart of man—that all religions have taught in different ways and different forms.

So many in this world only know the word "love"; to understand what love is or to speak about it or explain it is impossible. For whoever tries to express love makes an effort in vain; it is like trying to express God in words. Neither can God be expressed in words, nor love. There is a saying of a Persian poet who was an emperor, "I was destined to have so many slaves serving me, but from the moment love was born in my heart I became the slave of my every slave." The moment love is produced, that person does not need to go and find out where the Truth is; the Truth is born. For it is the loving one, the loving heart which is capable of understanding, of comprehending Truth. The reason is that the Truth is not outside of self, it is within us. For instance, when a person's heart is melted by a terrible suffering in life, it is then that what he says, or what he thinks, or what he does, in all is a fragrance of love. What is called in the Bible, "tongues of flame" or "words of flame," what are they? It rises when love has risen; it revivifies the thought, word, and action.

What, generally, man knows about love is the give and take: "If you give me twelve pence, I will give you a shilling." For as long as one sees life in the form of business, in the form of give and take, he does not know love, and it is a great pity, when, after knowing something of love, the heart has turned cold and bitter. And what reason is there? The reason is this, that when one digs the ground one must dig until the water comes. But if one digs halfway, then there is no water, there is mud.

But what is love? Love is a continual sacrifice. And what does sacrifice mean? Sacrifice means forgetting of the self. As Rumi says in his poem, the *Masnavi*: "The Beloved is all in all, the lover merely veils him. The Beloved is all that lives, the lover a dead thing." But what is this death? The death in life is life. Can anyone say, "I practice in life to be good," or "to be religious," without having the love element? But what use can his religion be if he is praying perhaps all day, or seems to be all goodness, if there is no love in his heart; what use is his religion to him?

The power of love is seen in all things, and in whatever form it acts, it shows a great virtue. One does not know always what power love has behind it, that there is nothing in the world which is more powerful than love. Think of the hen with its little chickens. At the time when they are so young that they seek her protection, if the horse came, if the elephant came, she would fight in defense.

And how man has abused the word *love*; how he uses in his false pretenses the word *love*! What happens is that man has made a false world and in this false world he is so absorbed that he cannot see the reality. It is for this that the saints and the sages and the up-raisers of mankind have been sent from time to time, because he is in a dream and he cannot awake from it. And of what does he dream? He dreams of this false world that he has created.

And what is religion? Religion is what breaks away the barriers of falsehood and guides man toward the Truth. What we call kindness, helpfulness, gentleness, meekness, or humility, what do all these virtues come from? Are they all not made of love? They are different forms of love. That shows that there is only one stream of virtue and that is love, and all different virtues that man knows, they are all different drops falling in different directions. And the idea of right and wrong, good and bad, we can find among all different people in different ways, but in love we all unite, whether from East or South, or West or North, for no one who is thoughtful will argue that cruelty is virtue and kindness a sin. Therefore, from the point of view of love we can all unite in one conception of good and bad, of right and wrong. All that is guided by the principle of love has its virtue, and all that is done by coldness, it is that which is wrong.

When we think of the condition through which humanity has passed in all different times—in the name of religion there have been wars and battles—one wonders if it was taught by the religion. Not at all; religion was the pretense, that men by this pretense wanted to cause bloodshed, absorbed in selfishness. And if ever there has been a kind of accusation against any religion in the world, it is not against the religion, it is against the misunderstanding of that religion by the followers of that religion.

Think of the life of the great Master Jesus Christ who was the soul of religion. One sees that from beginning to end there was nothing but love and forgiveness. The best expression of love is that love which is expressed in forgiveness. Those who came with their wrongs, errors, imperfections, before the love that was all forgiven; there was always a stream of love which always purified.

If people had followed the idea of forgiveness and of tolerance, humanity would not have come to the condition to which it has come today. The hatred and prejudice and bitterness that exist today between nations are beyond words to explain. And if there were one religion or a thousand religions, if that were to go on, one would doubt if there be a religion. It seems that man has now the profession of it, but what is needed is to live it. Why is humanity not coming together more? It is the lack of tolerance, the lack of forgiveness, it is the lack of love. And there may be a thousand different schemes that people will make in order to make the conditions better, and every effort made in that direction is worthwhile; but at the same time there remains a question: what effort would be most worthwhile? It is the waking of the divine Spirit which is called love, which has been buried in the heart of man. There are many political institutions, social institutions, and moral institutions, but what is most necessary today is the wakening of the religion of the heart. It does not matter what religion they profess if they know the depth of the religion, which is love. And then, all the different forms, the forms of religious service and the forms of prayer, behind them what secret is there? The secret is to prepare the heart for that bliss which only love can give.

The school of the Sufis, in whatever age, has been the school of the mystics. Its religion has been the religion of the heart, and it is therefore that there is a verse of Abul Allah, who says, "Qur'an, the Bible, or a martyr's cry, all these my heart can tolerate, since my religion is love alone." For the religion of love is the religion of tolerance, the religion of love is the religion of forgiveness.

The life in the world is such that it is as difficult for the rich as for the poor. A world such as this, made by falsehood, has its blows, continual blows, that a person of good heart has to stand. And there is only one safety from all these blows that might destroy the heart altogether: it is to learn how to tolerate, to learn how to forgive. For everyone says or does or thinks only according to his own particular evolution, and he cannot do better. Why not, therefore, tolerate? Why not, therefore, forgive? And if there is intolerance, then there must be a continual reciprocity; it is giving and taking intolerance. It means killing the element of love and giving life to the element which is death itself.

And if there is any inspiration, any revelation, that also is attained by a loving heart. The life's purpose is to make use of this shrine which is the human heart and which was made for God. And if there is a shrine and no God, the shrine is purposeless. And if there is a heart and the heart has not yet attained to that ideal, the only ideal which is worthy of love, that heart has not yet attained its purpose.

But no doubt it can be worthless if a person says, "I love God, but I do not love mankind." That profession is worthless. It is like saying, "Friend, I love you very much, but I cannot look at your face." The creation is the manifestation of God. It is in the art of the artist that we recognize Him. If we refuse to acknowledge the art, we do not know the Artist. The man who does not express his love, who does not forget himself in love, expressing it as respect, tolerance, and forgiveness, does not know religion.

Of course this is the first step, that one loves those one meets on the surface of the earth. Someone asked a great teacher if he would initiate him in mysticism. The great teacher answered, "Young man, have you ever loved?" The young man said, "I have not." The great teacher said, "Then go and love first; then come to me, that is the second step."

No doubt the love of the human being which is not progressive and has not developed to the love of God is not yet perfect. For love is for the real Beloved, Who really deserves it and Who alone deserves it. As children learn the lesson of home life by playing with dolls, so the soul that learns, learns in human love and completes his study in the love of God. And the love of God is that which is the purpose of the whole creation; if that were not the purpose, the creation would not have taken place. As the whole creation is from God, then it is of God. If it is of God, then it is the manifestation of love, and the manifestation of God is purposed to realize the perfection of love.

The Present
Need of the World

If one truly observes the present condition of humanity, no one with sense will deny the fact that the world today needs *the* religion. Why I say *the* religion, and not *a* religion, is because there are many religions existing today called *a* religion, but what is needed today is *the* religion. And now coming to the question what *the* religion must be—must it be a new religion? If it were a new religion, it could not be called *the* religion; then it would be like many religions. I call *the* religion that religion which one can see by rising above the sects and differences which divide men, and by understanding *the* religion we shall understand all religions which may be called a religion.

I do not mean that all the religions are not religion; they are the notes. But there is the music, and that music is *the* religion. Every religion strikes a note, a note which answers the demand of humanity in a certain epoch. But at the same time, the source of every note is the same music which manifests when the notes are arranged together. All the different religions are the different notes, and when they are arranged together they make music. You may ask why, at each epoch, all the music was not given; only a single note? The answer is that there are times in the life of an infant when a rattle is sufficient; for the violin another time in life comes. During the time of the Chaldeans, Arabs, Romans, Greeks, different religious ideals were brought. To the few, music was brought, to the many only a note. This shows that this music has always existed, only that man in general was not ready to grasp it, and so was given only one note. But the consequence was that the person who was given the C note and the other who was given the G note fought together, each saying, "The note given to me is the right note." There have always existed souls who have said, "G is right," and others who have said, "C is right." All are right notes, and when they are mixed together, then there is music. This shows that there is an outer substance of religion which is the form, and the inner essence which is wisdom. When wisdom has blessed the soul, then the soul has heard the divine music. And the words of Christ, "I am Alpha and Omega"—what do they mean? That it was only when He came as Jesus? No; that music belongs to Alpha and Omega, the First and the Last. Those who tuned their hearts to listen to music, who elevated their souls high enough, they heard this divine music. But those who played with their rattle, their unique note, they disputed one with the other. They would have refused a violin: they were not ready for it; they would not have known how to use it.

Today the world is starved more for religion than ever before. And what is the reason? The reason is that some simple souls, attached to the faith of their ancestors, held their faith with esteem, considering religion necessary in life; but many souls, with intelligence and reason and understanding of life, rebelled against religion, as the child, when grown up, throws away his rattle; he is no longer interested in it. So today the condition is that religion remains in the hands of those who have kept it in its outer form out of devotion and loyalty to their ancestors' faith; and those who are, so to speak, grown up in mind and spirit, and want something better, they can find nothing. Their souls hunger for music, and when they ask for music, they are given a rattle, and they throw away the rattle and say they do not care for music, the soul's music, and without it their life becomes empty. How few recognize this fact, and fewer still will admit it. The psychological condition of humanity has become such that a person with intelligence refuses the music. He does not want the music; he wants something, but he calls it by another name.

I will tell you my own experience in the Western world. Traveling for ten years, I have come in contact with people of intelligence, thinkers, men of science; and in them I have seen the greatest yearning for that religious spirit. They are longing every moment of their lives for it, for they find, with all their education and science, that there is some space empty in themselves and they want it filled. But, at the same time, if you speak of religion, they say, "No, no, speak of something else; we do not want religion." This means they know only the rattle part of religion and not the violin part. They do not think that a thing exists which can be different from a rattle and yet there is a perplexity in themselves, a spiritual craving, that is not answered even by all their learned and scientific pursuits.

Now, therefore, what is needed today in the world is reconciliation between the religious man and the one who runs away from religion. But what can we do when we see even in the Christian religion so many sects, one opposing another; and, besides the Christian, the Muslim religion, the Buddhist, Jewish, and many others, each considering their own and thinking the others not worth thinking about. Now to me these different religions are like different organs of the body, cut apart and thrown asunder.

Therefore, to me personally it seems as if one arm of the same person were cut off and rising to fight the other. Both are arms of the same person, and when this person is complete, when all these parts are brought together, then there is *the* religion.

Then what is the effort of the Sufi Movement? To make a new religion? No; it is to bring together the different organs of the one body, which is meant to be united and not thrown apart. You may ask what is our method. How do we work to bring about reconciliation? By realizing for ourselves that the essence of all religion is one, and that that essence is wisdom, and considering that wisdom to be our religion, whatever be our own form. The Sufi Movement has persons belonging to many different faiths among its members. Do you think they have given up their own religion? No. On the contrary, they are firmer in their own faith by understanding the faith of others. From the narrow point of view, fault may be found because they do not hate, mistrust, and criticize the religion of others. They have respect for the scriptures that millions of people have held as sacred, though those scriptures do not belong to their own religion. They desire to study and appreciate other scriptures, and so to find out that all wisdom comes from the one Source—the wisdom of the East and of the West. The Sufi Movement is therefore not a sect; it can be anything but a sect. And if it ever became one, it would be quite contrary to the idea with which it has been begun, because its main idea is to remove differences and distinctions which divide mankind. And this ideal is attained by the realization of the one Source of all human beings, and also the Goal, which we all call God.

The Coming World Religion

There are many prophecies and several beliefs on this subject, but what is most needed is to understand what religion means. The present religion, or the coming religion, or the past religion, are for those who divide the Truth, which is one, into many. In point of fact, what was is, and what is will be. Was this idea not supported by Jesus Christ, who said: "I have not come to give a new law; I have come to fulfill the law"? If Jesus Christ said this, who else can come out and say: "I give you a new religion"? There cannot be a new religion; one could as well say, "I wish to teach you a new wisdom." There cannot be a new wisdom; wisdom is the same, which was and is and always will be.

There arises a question in the heart of the inquirers, "Then what is this variety of religions which has engaged humanity for years in conflict with one another, so that most of the wars and battles were fought in the cause of religion?" This only shows the childish character of human nature. Religion which was given and is given, wherever it is given, religion which was given for unity, for harmony, for brotherhood, was used by childish human nature to fight and to dispute and to engage themselves in battles for years and years. And the most amusing thing for a thoughtful person is to think and see how this has given in the past history a most sacred character to war, to battle, and called it sacred war, or holy war. And the same tendency of making war with one another, which began in their religion, persisted in the time of materialism; the same tendency turned into war between nations. And, at the same time, the differences and distinctions which existed between the different faiths and beliefs still exist, and that prejudice and that difference and the bigotry which existed between nations, still exist in a smaller or greater degree. What does it show? It shows that the meaning of true religion has not been understood by the majority. Therefore, the mission that religion had to fulfill in connection with humanity still remains to be fulfilled. And it is at that fulfillment that Jesus Christ has hinted: "I have come to fulfill the law, not to give a new law."

Religion can be seen from five different points of view. The first, religion which is known to us as certain dogmas, laws, or teachings. And when we think and see the condition of the world, we see that the law is now given by the nation. Every nation now is responsible for the order and peace of the people.

Besides this, the second aspect of religion is the church and the form of the service. In this there are differences, and there will always be differences; it is a matter of temperament, it is a matter of tendency, and it also depends upon the customs and beliefs of the people who have inherited that tendency from their ancestors. Some have in their house of prayer different forms and different ceremonies which help them to feel elevated; the others have a simple service. The one appeals to the former and the other appeals to the latter.

No doubt the world is evolving to uniformity, and as now we see no very great difference between the forms, the form of everything—of different customs of greeting, of dressing, and many other things—so people are coming to a certain uniformity. At the same time, when we look at the subject from a different point of view, we shall find that uniformity very often takes away the beauty of life. In the countries so civilized and advanced, where the architecture and houses are all on the same plan, where all are dressed in the same way, people become so tired that they like to go to a different country and see houses distinct and different one from the other, and also the people. For instance, the method of writing music and the form of notation for the whole Western world is the same, but the distinction between the music of the French, Italians, Germans, Russians, gives a stimulus to the lover of music. And so it is in the distinctions of the forms. To want to make all people live alike and act all alike means to turn all people into the same form and same face, and what would happen then? The world would become very uninteresting. It is like tuning all the keys of the piano to the same note. It is not necessary to change the notes of the piano. What is necessary is to know the way of harmony, to know how to create harmony between the different notes.

The third aspect of religion is the religious ideal, the Lord and Master of religion, the Lord and Master that a soul has esteemed as the ideal. It is something which cannot be discussed, something which cannot be argued upon. The less spoken about it, the better it is. It is the outcome of the devotion of a sincere heart which gives birth to that ideal which is too sacred to mention, an ideal which cannot be compared, an ideal which cannot be explained. And when the followers of diverse religions come to this question and dispute over their ideals, the sacred ideals of which they have only some tradition—which they have not known, but of which they have only had a tradition—and wish to prove one better than the other, they merely lose time and they destroy that sacred sentiment which can only be preserved in the heart. The religious ideal is the medium by which one rises towards perfection. Whatever name a person gives to his ideal, that name is for him, and that name is most sacred for him. But that does not mean that that name limits that ideal. There is one ideal, the divine ideal. Call Him Christ, and let the same Christ be known by different names, given to Him by various communities. For instance, a person who has a great devotion, a great love and attachment for his friend, is speaking about friendship in high words, and he is saying what a sacred thing it is to become friends; but then there is another one who says: "Oh, I know your friend, what he is; he is no better than anybody else." The answer to this idea is given by Majnun, in the story told by the ancients, where someone said to Majnun, "Leila, your beloved, is not so beautiful as you think." He said, "My Leila must be seen with my eyes. If you wish to see how beautiful Leila is, you must borrow my eyes." Therefore, if you wish to regard the object of devotion of whatever faith, of whatever community, of whatever people, you will have to borrow their eyes, you will have to borrow their heart. There is no use in disputing over the points of history, over each tradition in history; they are often made by prejudice. Devotion is a matter of heart, and is made by the devotee.

The fourth aspect of religion is the idea of God. There will always be fights and discussions about it; one says, "The God of our family is one, and the God of your family is another." There have always been fights. In the old times there was a dispute between the people saying that the God of Beni Israel was a special God; and so every community and every Church made its God a special God. If there is a special God, it is not only a special God of a community, but a God of every individual. For man has to make his own God before he realizes the real God. But that God which man makes within himself becomes in the end the door by which he enters that shrine of his innermost being, the real God, Who is in the heart of man. And then one begins to realize that God is not a God of a certain community or people, but that God is the God of the whole Being.

And then we come to another aspect of religion, which is not necessarily the law or the ceremony or the divine ideal or God, but which is apart from all these four. That is, something living in the soul, in the mind, and in the heart of man, the absence of which keeps man as dead, and the presence of which gives him life. If there is any religion, it is that particular sense. And what is that sense? The Hindus have called it, in the Sanskrit language, *Dharma*, which, in the ordinary meaning of the word, is *duty*. But it is something much greater than what we know in our everyday life as duty. I do not call it *duty*, but *life itself*. When a person is thoughtful, when a person is considerate, when a person feels the obligations that he has towards his fellow man, towards his friend, towards his father or mother, or in whatever relation he stands to man, it is something living, it is something like water, which gives the sense of the living soul; the soul is not dead. It is this living soul which really makes a person alive. And the person who is not conscious of this, this tenderness, this sacredness of life, he lives, but the soul is in the grave. You do not need to ask that man what is his religion, what is his belief, for he is living it; life itself is his religion, and this is the true religion. The man conscious of honor, the man who has the sense of shame, who has the feeling of sincerity, whose sympathy, whose devotion is alive, that man is living, that man is religious.

It is this religion which has been the religion of the past and which will be the religion of the future. And religion, if ever it was taught by Christ or any other great ones, was to awaken in man that sense which is awakened when this religion is living.

It does not matter into which house you go and pray, for every moment of your life then is religion. Then it is not a religion in which you believe, but it is a religion which you live.

What is the Message of Sufism? Sufism is the Message of digging out that water-like life, which has been buried by the impressions of this material life. There is an English phrase: "A lost soul." The soul is not lost; the soul is buried. When it is dug out, then the divine life springs out like a spring of water. And the question is, what is digging? What does one dig in oneself? Is it not true, is it not said in the scriptures, that God is love? Then where is God to be found? Is He to be found in the seventh heaven or is He to be found in the heart of man? He is to be found in the heart of man, which is his shrine. But if this heart is buried—the heart which has lost that light, that life, that warmth—what does this heart become? It becomes as a grave. There is in a popular song in English a beautiful line which says: "The light of the whole life dies when love is done." That living thing in the heart is love. It may come as kindness, as friendship, as sympathy, as tolerance, as forgiveness—in whatever form this living water rises from the heart, it proves the heart to be a divine spring. And when once this spring is open and is rising, everything that man does as an action, as a word, as a feeling, it is all religion; that man becomes religious.

If there is any coming religion, a new religion to come, it will be this religion, *the religion of the heart*. After all the suffering that has been caused to humanity by the recent war, man is beginning to open his eyes. And as time will pass he will open his eyes to know and understand that the true religion is in opening the heart, in widening the outlook, and in living the religion which is one religion.

The Sufi's Religion

Religion in the ordinary sense of the word, as known by the world, is the creeds. There are not many religions in the world, but there are many creeds. And what does creed mean? Creed means a cover over the religion. There is one religion and there are many covers. Each of these covers has a name: Christianity, Buddhism, Judaism, Islam, etc., and when you take off these covers, you will find that there is one religion, and it is that religion which is the religion of the Sufi. And at the same time, a Sufi does not condemn a church or creed or a certain form of worship. He says it is the world of variety. Everyone must have his choice of food, his choice of dress, his choice of expression. Why must the followers of one faith think that the others are heathens or pagans? The Sufi thinks that we all follow one religion, only in different names, and different forms; but behind names and forms there is one and the same spirit and there is one and the same truth. The pity is that the orthodox priests and clergy disagree among themselves about it; even in the colleges and in the universities, when students study theology, they study without interest. A professor told me in Switzerland that "we have read many books of religion. I was a professor of theology; but we are taught in the college to study without taking deep interest in the subject, to be neutral." But that is not the attitude to become inspired. Our attitude must be that of interest, of sympathy, of friendliness toward that religion and toward the Teacher who has brought it.

I began to study the Bible in my early youth and my devotion towards Christ and the Bible was as great as that of any Christian, or perhaps more. And so it is with all scriptures. If you have sympathy, if you have interest in all you study and read, then it is living, then it inspires you, you are benefited by it because of your love for truth. The same truth is common to all, but the tendency of the academic study of religion is to find where the differences are. They would be most interested in knowing where Christianity differs from Buddhism and where the Jewish religion differs from Islam. Their interest is in the difference instead of in the synthesis, where we meet. It is in the meeting ground of different faiths that there is the sacred place of pilgrimage. In India, in order to teach this idea, they have made a place of pilgrimage where two rivers meet. When there is one river, they call it sacred, but the most sacred place is where two rivers meet. It is the same thought that every stream of Divine Wisdom which we call religion is sacred, but most sacred it is there where two streams meet. And when we realize that, we make the real pilgrimage in the spirit.

And now, coming to the idea of what religion consists of. The first thing in religion is the idea of God. What is God? Some say that "my idea of God is that He is in the highest Heaven, that He is the Creator, that He is the Judge of the Last Day, that He is the Forgiver." And there is another one who says: "My idea is that God is all, God is abstract, all is God, and if anyone believes in a personal God, I do not believe it." Both are right and yet both are wrong. They are right if they see the other point of view and they are wrong if they see their own point of view. Both see the God-ideal with one eye. One sees it with the right eye and the other with the left eye. If they see with both eyes, then the vision is complete. It is indeed an error on the part of man to limit God in the idea of a Personal Being, and is wrong in the person who believes in the Absolute God to efface the Being of God from his conception of it. As they say: "To explain God is to dethrone God." To say that God is abstract is like saying: "God is space, God is time." Can you love space? Can you love time? There is nothing there to love. A beautiful flower would attract you more than space. And nice music will attract you more than time. Therefore the believer in the abstract God has only his belief, but he is not benefited by it. He may just as well believe in no God as in an abstract God. Yet he is not wrong. He is uselessly right.

The most advisable thing for the believer of God is to first make his own conception of God. Naturally man cannot make a conception of something he does not know. For instance, if I told you to imagine a bird that you have never seen, which is unlike any bird you have ever seen, you would first attach to the bird wings, then you might see the head of a cow, and then perhaps you would imagine the feet of a horse and a peacock's tail. But you cannot imagine any form which you have not seen, which you have not known. You have to embody from your mind a form which you already know. You cannot make a conception which you have never seen or known before. Besides, it is the easiest thing and it is the most natural thing for man to conceive of any being in his own form. When man thinks of fairies or angels he sees them in human form, and therefore if a person conceives of the God-ideal, even the highest and best way of conceiving will be in the highest and best human personality. There is nothing wrong about it. That is all that man can do. God is greater than man's conception, but man cannot conceive Him higher than he can. Therefore, any man's God is in his own conception. It is useless, therefore, to argue and to discuss and to urge one's own conception upon another. For the.best way a person can think of God is in the way he is capable of thinking of God.

And then the next aspect of religion is the ideal of the Teacher. One says that: "My teacher is the Savior of the world, the Savior of humanity. My Teacher is divine, my Teacher is God Himself." And there is another who is ready to oppose it, saying that it is not true, no man can be called divine and no one can save the world, each one has to save himself. But if you look at it from the Sufi's point of view, the Sufi says: "What does it matter if a man sees in someone he adores and worships and idealizes, God Himself? After all, this whole manifestation is God's manifestation. If he says that in that particular Teacher he sees the Divine, there is nothing wrong about it. Let him call his Teacher Divinity. I am sorry for the one who does not call his Teacher the Savior." Besides that, we each have an effect of our deeds on the whole cosmos and if a high soul was called by someone "the Savior of the World," it is not an exaggeration. One wicked soul can cause such harm to the whole cosmos, and one holy soul by his life on earth can do so much good, directly and indirectly, to each being in the world, because each soul is connected with the whole cosmos. But for the Sufi there is no dispute about it. If a Buddhist says: "Buddha is my Savior," if a Christian says that Christ is divine, if a Muslim says that Muhammad was the Seal of the Prophets, if a Hindu says that Krishna was the expression of God, the Sufi says: "You are all justified; you each have your name, individually or collectively. You are calling my Ideal. All these names are the name of my Ideal. You each have your own ideals. I have all these names as the name of my Ideal. I call my Beloved: Krishna, Buddha, Christ, Muhammad. Therefore all your ideals I love, because my ideal is one and the same."

And now comes the third idea in religion, and that is the idea of the form of worship. Perhaps in one religion there are candles lighted and there is a form of worship. And there is another religion where even a song is not allowed to be sung in the church. In another religion they call out the name of God and pray the Lord with movements. In another religion they have put a statue of Buddha on the altar as the sign of peace. These are different expressions of devotion. Just as in the Western countries by nodding and in the Eastern countries by raising their hands, they salute one another. It is the same feeling, but the action is different. What does it matter if one greets in this way or in that way; is it not all a greeting? The Sufi says, so long as there is real devotion, it does not matter in what way it is expressed. For him it is the same.

Once I was traveling from England to the United States, and on the ship on Sunday there was a Protestant service, which I attended, and everyone thought I was a Protestant. Then there was a Catholic service, and when I went to the Catholic service, people began to look at me, doubting if I was a Catholic or a Protestant. After that, there was a Jewish service, and when I went, they began to think that, if I was a Rabbi, why did I go to all these services? To me every one of these services was an expression of devotion; for me they were not different. The form makes no difference, it is our feeling. When our feeling is right, if we are in the church or in the marketplace or in simple nature or in our own house, we always will express our sincere devotion. Therefore a Sufi's form of prayer is all forms of prayer, and in every form he feels that exaltation which is the principal thing to experience in religious life.

There is another aspect of religion, which is what is forbidden and what is allowed, the moral and ethical conception. One religion says, this is forbidden and this is allowed; another religion says another thing and another religion still another thing. But what is this law? Where does it come from? This law comes from the conception of the Prophets or law-givers which they have gotten from the need of the community. And therefore, perhaps, one law-giver was born in Syria, another in Arabia, another in India, another in China, and each one saw a different need for the people of that time. And therefore if we gather together the laws the religious inspirers have given, they naturally will differ if we dispute over them, saying that my religion is better and yours is worse because its laws are better and yours are worse. It is a foolish thing to do. If one nation says, "Our law is better than your law and your law is worse than ours," there is no meaning in it, because nations make their laws according to their needs. The needs of every race and community and nation, sometimes, are different. Nevertheless, the fundamental principle is one and the same. To have consideration for another is the root of all the religious laws. To feel, "I am in the same position as another; if I act unjustly to another, the other is also entitled to act unjustly to me. I am exposed to the same thing." When this thought is awakened in man and sympathy is awakened for his fellow men, he need not trouble and argue and discuss about the different laws.

Friends, love is a great inspirer of law, and the one who has not love, he may read a thousand books of law, he will always accuse others of their faults and he will never know his own faults. But if love has wakened in your heart, then you do not need to study law, for you know the best law, for all law has come from love and still love stands above law.

People say that there will be justice in the hereafter and we shall all have to show the accounts of our deeds. In the first place, we ourselves do not know the account of our deeds. Besides, if God is so exacting as to ask you of every little evil everyone has a committed, then God must be worse than man, because even a fine man overlooks his friend's faults, a kind man forgives a person's faults. If God is so exacting as that, He must be an autocratic God. It is not true; God is not Law, God is Love. Law is the law of nature, but God's Being is not Law, God's Being is Love. And therefore the right conception of life and insight into right and wrong, good and bad, is not learned and taught by book-study. As the Sufi says: all virtues manifest by themselves once the heart is wakened to love and kindness.

Another aspect of religion is the sacred shrines, the importance that one attaches to the church or priest or clergyman or to a certain house of prayer, to the temple, pagoda, mosque or synagogue. For the Sufi, it is not the place that is holy, but it is our faith that makes it so; and if a person has faith that this place, this synagogue, temple or church is holy, he will be benefited by it. But, at the same time, the holiness is not in the house, the holiness is in his own belief. But what we have to learn from religion is one thing, and that is the knowledge of Truth. At the same time, Truth cannot be spoken in words. Truth is something that is discovered, not learned and taught. The great mistake is that people confuse fact and Truth; therefore, they neither know about Truth nor about fact. Besides, there are many who are so sure of their truth that they hammer that truth upon another. They say: "I do not mind if you are hurt or if you are vexed, I just tell you the truth." Such hammered truth cannot be the Truth. It is a hammer. Truth is too delicate, too tender, too beautiful. Can Truth hurt anyone? If Truth was so dense and gross, sharp and hurtful, it could not be Truth. Truth stands above words. Words are too rigid to express Truth. Even such fine feelings as tenderness, gentleness, sympathy, love, gratitude, Truth is above them. Truth cannot be explained. Truth is above all emotion, above all passion. Truth is a realization, a realization which cannot be put into words because language has no words to express it. What are facts? Facts are the shadows of Truth. They give an illusion of Truth. And people dispute over facts, and in the end they find nothing.

And now the question is, how can one attain to Truth by what is called Religion? And I say, all aspects of religion help one to attain to Truth if they are understood rightly. The first aspect is God; God is like a steppingstone, God is like a key to Truth, and if a person keeps the ideal of God away and wishes to come to the realization of Truth, he misses a great deal in life. He may come to a certain conception of Truth, but he has taken the wrong way just the same; he has wandered about; he could have come by the right way.

And the second thing is the thought of the Teacher whom one idealizes. Why must we not have a high conception of the Divine in man? It is the most beautiful thing one can have, and the one who has not the high conception of a human being born in any age, in the past or in the present, that one is missing a great deal in life. It is a need of the soul to have a high ideal, an ideal which one can conceive of as a human being.

I will tell you a little experience I had in this matter. A girl was working in a factory and she was so religious that she always had the Bible with her, and the name of Christ would make tears come from her eyes. And the scientific director of that factory came to this girl, simple and devotional and knowing no science or philosophy. He said to her: "You seem to be very religious." "No," she said, "for me Christ is everything. That is all I know." And he said: "But there never was a man born as Christ; look here, this is the book of a great clergyman." He showed her. He said: "You are what they call a religious fanatic. You will get a religious mania." And this poor girl did not know where she was and she did not know what to believe and what not to believe; she was, so to speak, lost in the mist. The idea of a religious mania! A material man who has no religion, but believes only in science, he also has a mania. Is there not a material mania? For many, money is all that is. They have lost their religion, and their brain and thought is for money. All their life they only know of making money. And that is a mania, a material mania, which is worse than the religious mania. Religious mania lasts after death, but the material mania cannot be cured by it. What the material people cannot understand is that they themselves suffer from a mania, and if you ask them if they know about themselves, you will find that they have a great mania which they do not know. They know about everybody, but they do not know about themselves.

This girl from that day gave up food; she could not eat, she could not go to sleep. She said: "I do not know where I am. This one thing in my life I believed in and looked forward to, has been taken away. Now I do not know what to believe and not to believe." This girl was brought to me and when I told her that the one who said, "This is a mania," he has a material mania, she understood. I said: "No doubt your devotion has a greater reality than all the realities that are outside," and she understood. Thought and feeling are more real than what is outside. Therefore an object of devotion in religion is always a most comforting thing.

And then coming to the form of worship. We have a body and since we ourselves have a form, we cannot condemn the idea of form. Besides, the life we live, it is all form, although it is illusion. But at the same time we cannot live without it. Since we have form for all material things, why may we not have a form for our prayer? There is nothing wrong about it.

And the fourth thing is the moral principle. It is natural that we must have a principle in our life whether this principle or that principle. We must have some principle for which we shall sacrifice our benefit in life.

And the fifth thing is the realization of Truth. And that realization comes by itself once we give ourselves to the seeking after

Truth, because Truth is our very Self. And it is the realization of Self which is the realization of Truth.

Seeking for the Ideal

Religion is a need of the human soul. In all periods and at every stage of the evolution of humanity there has been a religion followed by the world. At whatever stage of evolution, and in whatever period, the need for religion has been felt. And the reason is, that the soul of man has five deep desires, and these desires are answered by religion.

The first desire is the seeking for the ideal. There comes a time when man seeks for a more complete justice than he finds among men, and when he seeks for someone on whom he can rely more surely than he can on his friends in the world. There comes a time when one feels a desire to open his heart to a Being who is above human beings and who can understand his heart. Man naturally desires to meet someone who is greater than he. And when he seeks his ideal in the world of mortality, since the human soul cannot come up to his ideal he is naturally inclined to turn towards Someone who is higher than man. Man wants to feel that there is Someone who comes to his aid, Someone who is near him in his loneliness. He feels the need of asking forgiveness of Someone who is above human littleness, and of seeking refuge under Someone stronger than he. And to all these natural human tendencies there is an answer, and the answer is given by religion, and the answer is God.

Every living being on earth loves life above all else. The smallest insect, whose life lasts only an instant, tries to escape from any danger in order to live a moment longer. And the desire to live is most awakened in man. As intelligence wakens in man, he begins to wonder whether life is merely transitory, and if, after this life, all is ended. The thought that, "After my short life the world will continue; it will live"—this thought, for a man, is more terrible than death. And if life had not an intoxicating effect, this thought would kill many people. The man who thinks that after this life there is nothing more, cannot dwell very long on that thought. Dwelling on this thought and contemplating upon it is like what a man feels who is standing on a great height and looks down—it terrifies him. The belief that life will continue after we have gone through death is a most comforting idea for every soul. The man who has not received the reward of his efforts, of his goodness; who has not, in his life, met with an answer to the sense of justice in him; who has not found in life a complete satisfaction; the man who has not been able to attain his desire in life—his hope is in what will come after, and this religion promises him.

Man has a desire for exaltation, the exaltation that is afforded him by cleanliness of body and purity of mind. Man longs to feel exalted both by the power of words and by his surroundings. And man strives for exaltation by thought, by action, and by feeling. The nature of life in the world is such that it constantly drags man to the earth. His senses continually draw him towards the earth: the crudeness of human nature, which jars continually, draws man towards the earth, bearing constantly the heavy burden of human responsibilities, and realizing in the end that these responsibilities are not of great importance. And the only change one can bring about to rid oneself of material responsibilities, is by prayer, either by oneself or joining with others in religious rites and ceremonies that afford man the means of exaltation in answer to his desire.

Man, with the maturity of his soul, desires to probe the depths of life. He desires to discover the power latent within him, he longs to know the source and goal of his life, he yearns to understand the aim and meaning of life, he wishes to understand the inner significance of things, and he wants to uncover all that is covered by form and name: he seeks for insight into cause and effect, he wants to touch the mystery of Time and Space, and he wishes to find the missing link between God and man—where man ends, where God begins. And this desire also finds its fulfillment in the contact with the spirit that religion gives.

It is a most natural desire of the human soul to seek for happiness and comfort. Man desires principles to guide his life, and he wishes for a moral standard to regulate the life of the community. He wishes for a balance of activity and repose; he desires union with the one whom he loves; he wishes for security of all that belongs to him, a settled reciprocity, a fixed give-and-take, and all things which bring about happiness and peace at home and in the nation.

Today, in the world, many people think that one can do without religion, and that they themselves have outgrown religion by reason of their evolution. Many have no religious belief. And therefore the world has never been in a more chaotic condition. No doubt one finds in tradition and in history that in the name of religion the selfishness and ignorance of mankind has played a great part. Therefore man, revolting against this state of things, has forsaken religion, and has forgotten that spirit which, in the name of religion, has also played its part in the world. And now, in the absence of the influence of religion, the spirit which in the name of religion played a part in history has continued to play its part under the name of modernism. In spite of the separation that man tries to make between himself and others, he has always felt in himself a lack, at home and in his country. And this can be seen, today, among the materialists, who would not for one moment allow themselves to have a religious belief, but yet they are not satisfied. And the reason is that they lack a very great and very important thing, a thing that they cannot attain because they have built a wall before themselves.

There is a desire in every person, be he happy or unhappy. That desire is to live; even if not on the earth, in the hereafter. And the one who looks at it with pessimism and says, "I do not know if there is a hereafter," he also would like to be convinced that there is a hereafter. If that person disputes with you against the possibility of the hereafter, it is only to establish in his mind a conviction that there is a hereafter. He will not admit it, for he thinks it is intelligence to deny it. But he is not willing to die: he is not willing to deny that there is a continual life.

The mission of devotion, of religion, of spirituality, therefore, has been to bring that conviction to man which outer reasoning denies, but belief and faith alone can give. Is there one person in this world who would like that his existence should cease for good? Not one person. But every person seemingly or unseemingly is in the pursuit of finding out, if he can, some thread, some link, in order to be sure that there is a life in the hereafter. It is not true that there is no proof of the hereafter; only, those who want a proof, they look for that proof in a wrong direction. How can a proof of immortality be found in mortal existence? The proof of immortality is immortality itself. As life has no experience, it has no proof. If there is a proof, it is life itself. It is just like wakening from unconsciousness and coming to consciousness; so it is coming to immortality from the limited conception of mortality. Has not every religion tried in its own way, by giving some means or the other, to bring man to realize that there is a life in the hereafter?

It is the present age which objects to believing something which can only be understood in its culmination; and that way it refuses to believe it. Belief, when it is developed, is faith. And it is in that faith that you will find a seal; by opening it, there is a revelation of the continuity of life. No one but one's own self can convince one of the life in the hereafter; but one can give oneself a belief to begin with: the conviction will come by itself. Many have taken wrong methods in order to convince man of the hereafter. And by trying to play with phenomena they have, instead of giving a new belief, taken away the belief of the intelligent and built a wrong belief in the simple ones.

The work of the Sufi Message, therefore, is to use all different methods, devotional, religious, spiritual, which will suit the particular grade of a person's evolution, in order to prepare his heart for that conviction which is called the life immortal.

Law

"I have not come to give a new law, I have come to fulfill the law," said Christ. This suggests two things. One is that to give a law is one of the principal objects of the coming of the Messenger. In the traditions of the past we see that it was what is called the divine law that governed the nations. And even now the law is necessarily based on a religious principle, which shows us that even in earthly things the divine guidance has always been considered most necessary. The worldly-wise do not know spiritual things, whereas the spiritually-wise are wise in earthly things also. And Christ, whose life was free from earthly thought, withdrawn from the world even, it is He who has given to the people of His time the divine law. Krishna, with all His philosophical and mystical ideas, speaks of the law of worldly life. Today a Muslim follows most respectfully the law given by his Prophet, and recognizes with pride that his Prophet had in his life military service and political responsibilities, and that his Prophet was at the same time a man of the world and a man of God. To whatever extent the world may evolve, a thoughtful man will never be able to deny the fact that it is not for everyone, for every mind, to touch the depths of thought. Whether there be aristocracy or democracy, there will always be a few souls who will have influence over many. We see that all men are different, each has his own way to follow, and no one can fill the place of another. If it happens that in worldly affairs there is what is called the man of the moment, then even in spiritual affairs there may be the soul of the age. The Messengers who have brought the law have been the Messengers of their time, but, since today man knows only the earthly affairs, he concerns himself little with the affairs of the soul. As he concerns himself little with this question, he is very little aware of what happens in spiritual conditions; nevertheless the work of God and of creation pursues its course just the same. The Spirit, which is called Alpha and Omega, is always present and is always doing its work, recognized or unrecognized.

We can see the law in five aspects. First, the institution of marriage and of divorce is the first thing necessary for the peace of the world. This law is necessary to safeguard in life the rights of woman, whose position is more delicate than that of man. The recognition given to marriage by the law makes an impression upon the two persons, pointing out that they are connected by law and by religion. The necessity of divorce, a thing that is sometimes necessary to put an end to the captivity of two persons who cannot agree in living together, also is a part of the law. If there were not a religious influence—if one had not the impression, *Our marriage is made before God*—it would very much lessen the seriousness with which marriage is viewed. For instance, today there is a way of marrying which has nothing to do with religion, and often marriage becomes simply a matter of the law courts. One can imagine how man considers this question when it is a question that can be settled in the court. Nothing in the world can take the place, in marriage, of what religion gives to marriage.

The second aspect is the division of property and the manner of safeguarding property. The law of religion, with the justice of God, teaches man to regard the rights of others as well as his own rights. Besides, religion teaches what one may rightfully call one's own, and what ought not to belong to us. It teaches also how one should earn money, and how one should spend it. The serious aspect of religion, the thought of God and of Truth which is behind all this, creates in life that spirit of honesty which religion is meant to create.

Third, there are birth and death. At the coming of the child, the thought of spiritual illumination in some form or other, to welcome him on earth—this necessarily makes a foundation for spiritual development in the life of the infant; and, in the family in which the child arrives, the feeling that he has come as a gift from God, the thought that: "We, the parents, are not alone responsible for this child's life; behind there is God, Who shares our responsibility."

At the death of a person, a religious ceremony performed gives strength to the one who is passing from this world into another world, and it is also a consolation to those who think of him with love. For it brings the thought that the dead one is called towards the Source whence he has come. And, besides, added to the thought which comes with death, the religious ceremony creates also in the minds of those present the thought: "We are not here permanently. Life is like a caravan. All have to go along the same road. One goes first; the others follow in their turn." Think what a virtue this thought brings us! It makes the fact of this illusory world pale, which yet keeps so many engaged day and night in its pursuit. It offers man an opportunity to be still for a moment and consider life, man who is always absorbed in the affairs of this world of illusion.

The fourth aspect that the law of religion represents is social life. People meeting in a church, at a meeting for a service or a religious ceremony, naturally gives the opportunity of joining together in the thought of God and of religion. Places of pilgrimage and sacred places, all this unites humanity in the love of God and in unity. Think of people gathered together at an exhibition, a fair; the feeling that animates them all is gain, to get the best of the bargain. What an incomparable difference when one meets in a sacred and religious thought!

The fifth institution is the political institution of the religious law—all that concerns the community or the country; a law which, with divine justice, concerns itself with the affairs of the community and the affairs of the country. A problem, which cannot be solved otherwise, can be solved by spiritual enlightenment. Man is naturally selfish, and justice cannot exist in the heart in which there is the thought of self. That one alone can look at things from a just point of view whose heart reflects God absolutely—God, Who is above nation, race, caste, creed, or religion.

No doubt, where there is truth there is also untruth, where there is day there is also night. It is natural that often the religious authorities have abused the law. When a spiritual man concerns himself with the things of the world, it is extremely difficult for him not to allow the things of the world to throw their shadow on his heart. Men, revolted by the abuse of religion, have often given up religion itself, and it is this that has made man ignorant of the divine source of the law that rules the affairs of the world. Today man thinks that to make laws is the work of intellectual people. This brings constant disappointments both to nations and to communities. The lack of order and peace throughout the world today, one may say, is caused by the want of the law which must come from God, from the divine source. Man is too small to be able to find the solution of the problems of this world. That is the work of the perfect wisdom which is found in a Personality without limitations, with which human personality cannot be compared, as one cannot compare a drop with the ocean.

Prayer

Often mankind thinks, "Since God is the knower of the heart of every man, what does it matter if prayer is recited and gesture or action made? Would it not be sufficient if one sat in silence and thought of God?" And the answer is that it is according to the extent of your consciousness of prayer that your prayer reaches God. If your body is silent and only your mind working, part of your being is praying and part is not, for you are constituted of both mind and body. Therefore, when the mind is praying the body must pray too, to make it complete. In reality God is within you, and as He is within you, you are the instrument of God and through you God experiences the external world and you are the best instrument of conveying yourself to God. Therefore your thought, action and word makes prayer complete.

Then there is another idea. The next question is, when God already knows what we want, what is good for us, what we need, why should we ask Him for it? He knows it. For this in the first place I would quote Christ's words: "Knock, and it shall be opened unto you; ask, and ye shall receive." In other words God knows your need, He knows what you want, but your want becomes clear when it is expressed not by the mind or the body only, but by your whole being. That is the secret.

The question, "Why does God need praise from us? Who are we that we should praise God?" is answered thus: We can never praise Him enough, and our praise can never be sufficient, but at the same time our soul is blessed with the impression of the Glory of God whenever we praise Him. The soul could praise God every moment and yet be wanting to praise Him more. It is constantly hungering and thirsting to find the perfection of beauty. When to our utmost we praise the beauty of God, our soul is filled with bliss. Even to utter the name of God is a bliss which fills the soul with light and joy and happiness as nothing else can.

The first aspect of prayer is giving thanks to God for all the numberless blessings that are bestowed upon us at every moment of the day and night, of which man is mostly unconscious.

The second aspect of prayer is laying one's shortcomings before the unlimited Perfection of the Divine Being, and asking His forgiveness.

This makes man conscious of his smallness, of his limitedness, and therefore makes him humble before his God. And by humbling himself before God man does not lose any virtue. God alone has the right to demand complete humility. There is another side to this question: although humility is painful to the pride of man, the joy of humility is never known by the proud. The effect produced upon his own feeling is as if, by his very humility, he had opened the doors of the shrine of God which is in the heart of man. The one who asks forgiveness of his friend feels a joy that he of whom it is asked does not know. And it must not be forgotten that it is not pride that gives joy, but it is humility which gives a special joy.

If we can only know the joy of asking pardon even of our fellow man, when we realize we are in fault, however little it may be! And when we ask the Father of all to forgive our fault, joy, beauty, happiness, spring up in the heart in a way unknown until it is experienced. And then to think we can ask pardon of Him Whose love is unlimited, while our errors are numberless and our ignorance limitless! Think of the joy of asking forgiveness from God! Every moment of our life, if we can see wisely, contains some fault or error, and asking pardon is just like purifying the heart and washing it white. Only think of the joy of humbling yourself before God! There is a story told of Akbar. He was mourning for the death of his mother and for a long time his grief was so great he could not overcome it. His ministers and friends tried to comfort him, telling him how fortunate he was, how great was his influence and power. He answered, "Yes, I know it, but one thing grieves me. I have everyone to bow before me, but there was one, when I came in the palace, before whom I could be humble. I could be as nothing before her and I cannot tell you the joy of that."

Think then of the greater joy of humbling yourself before that Spirit, that Ideal, who is the true Father and Mother, on Whose love you can always depend; it is a spark of His love which expresses itself in the earthly father and mother, and in whatever manner you humble yourself before Him, it can never be enough. To humble your limited self before His Perfection, that is to deny yourself. Self-denial is not renouncing things, it is denying the self, and its first lesson is humility.

And the blessing one can receive by prayer becomes a thousand fold greater when that blessing is received by some few who are united in the same thought and are praying together.

Humility has several forms, and these forms are observed according to the customs of different peoples. There are forms of respect known: towards parents, towards Teachers, Masters. But at the end of examination, and after studying life keenly, one finds that it is to God alone that all forms of respect are addressed. And it is this lesson that the different religions have given to different peoples according to their needs.

And the third aspect of prayer is to tell to God one's difficulties, the troubles of one's life, and to ask God for what one needs and one wants. And who else deserves this trust but God? It is true that we have relations, friends who love us and wish to help us. But they are only human beings, traveling in the same boat on the same sea, subject to all the same difficulties, the same limitations. And man can be helped by man only to a certain extent. The more one studies human nature, the more one feels inclined to bring before God alone one's troubles, one's difficulties, and one's sorrows. Therefore this is a part of what is taught in the form of prayer: it is called an aspect of prayer.

The fourth aspect of prayer is the call of the lover to the beloved. No doubt this is a higher form; and to be able to pray in this manner man must rise above the ordinary level of life. As it is difficult for a human being to love man, whom he sees, so it is more difficult to love God, Whom one has never seen. Loving one's fellow man, yes; but not everyone is capable of loving the Formless, the God-Ideal, and to evolve by the lesson of love. For in this love there is no disappointment, and only the love of God can fulfill the desire of the human soul, and all other forms of love are only as steps that lead to the love of God. But who can explain the love of God to one who has never felt it? Because God is the perfect ideal, His love is the perfect love. There is the love of the mate, of parents, of friends, of children, but in the love of God all is found combined.

Therefore its joy is perfect. The love of God is living and everlasting and the love of the true Beloved.

The fifth aspect of prayer is to know God, and by this means to draw nearer to God, which is the real meaning of the word "at-one-ment," which means complete union. And this cannot be learned; it is a natural tendency: it is the attraction of the soul to God. It is as the negative pole of the electric wire is attracted to the positive. Which means that the happiness of man depends on his nearness to God. This has been taught in the form of prayer.

It is these five aspects of prayer which constitute the form of religious worship. Every religion, at whatever time and in whatever country it has been given, has given as its method prayer. But man has always shown his childish nature. He has always fought with his neighbor because he does not pray as he himself does. Man has taken the outer form of prayer. He has used the outer form of prayer to satisfy his vanity, and the consequence has been that man, revolted by this state of things, has given up prayer. For instance, Protestantism is a sort of protest against the Catholic form of prayer. Many people, between the two, have given up prayer. And giving it up is not satisfactory, for nothing can take the place of what is called prayer.

The chaotic condition at the present time is caused by the lack of religion. Man's soul needs religion: his mind fights against it. In history we find that most wars have been caused by disputes about religion. In the East no one dares to say that he does not believe in God. In the West there are people who are proud of not believing in God. They say: "Force, or forces, are the origin of life." It is the greatest tragedy if one deprives oneself of God, because there cannot be any other means for man of rising to a higher consciousness.

The question arises in the inquiring mind: If God is within man, all our troubles and difficulties, our feelings and our attitude towards Him, our faults, are known to Him—what need is there to express them in prayer? It is like saying, "Because I love a certain person, why should I show it?" *Expression is the nature of life.* When every part of man's mind and body expresses his feeling, his thought, his aspiration, then it produces its full effect. And no doubt, by the fact of being met together for prayer, the effect is greater. The blessing that one can receive through prayer becomes a thousand fold greater when received by a few united in the same thought, and who are praying together.

Besides, the psychological effect is another thing. The world is a dome, and in this dome, every word that is uttered resounds. And when the resonance is produced in this dome, its re-echo is produced, and what comes, comes as the answer of God.

The question whether God has time to give attention to our prayer is answered, by the mystic, that it is through the medium of man himself that God hears his prayer. In the East the head of man is called the dome of God, which means "the greatest secret" and also "the highest place." For outwardly, it is the head which represents the eternal abode. It is for this reason that it is said in the scriptures, "We have created man in Our own Image."

The Effect of Prayer

There are three kinds of people among those who are in the habit of offering prayer.

There is one person who by praying fulfills a certain duty, which he considers as one among all the other duties of life. He does not know to whom he is praying; he thinks to some God. If he is in the congregation, he feels of necessity obliged to do as the others do. He is like one among the sheep who goes on, he does not know where and why. Prayer, to him, is something that he must do because he is put in a situation where he cannot help it. In order to fall in with the custom of the family or community, and in order to respect those around him, he does it as everybody else. His prayer is mechanical, and, if it makes any effect, it is very little.

And the second kind of person who offers his prayers is the one who offers the prayers because he is taught to do so, and yet is confused as to whether there is any God, if his prayers are really heard. He may be praying, and at the same time confusion may be going on in his mind: "Am I doing right or wrong?" If he is a busy man, he might think, "Am I giving my time to something really profitable, or am I wasting it? I see no one before me. I hear no answer to my prayer." He does it because he was taught by someone to do it, or because perhaps it might bring him some good. His prayer is a prayer in the dark. The heart, which must be opened to God, is covered by his own doubt, and if he prayed in this way for a thousand years, it is never heard. It is this kind of soul who in the end loses his faith, especially when he meets with a disappointment. He prays, and if his prayer is not answered, that puts an end to his belief.

Then there is a third person who has imagination which is strengthened by faith. He does not only pray to God, but he prays before God, in the presence of God. Once imagination has helped man to bring the presence of God before him, God in his own heart is wakened. Then, before he utters a word, it is heard by God; when he is praying in a room, he is not alone, he is there with God; then God to him is not in the highest heaven, but next to him, before him, in him; then heaven to him is on earth, and the earth for him is heaven; no one to him is then so living as God, so intelligible as God, and the names and forms before him, all are covered under Him. Then every word of prayer he utters is a living word. It does not only bring him blessing, but blessings to all those around him. It is this manner of prayer which only is the right way of praying, and by this manner the object that is to be fulfilled by prayer is accomplished.

～

It is not only belief but faith which is necessary. Belief is a thing, but faith is a living being. We rise by treading the path of faith. Someday we shall realize what God is, but that only comes after the first lesson has been learned. Faith is the A B C of the revelation of God. This faith is begun by prayer.

There are two ways of prayer, and in the first way there are three kinds of prayer.

～

One prayer is thanksgiving to God for His great goodness, for all that we receive in our life; asking God for His mercy and favor and forgiveness; asking God to grant the desires and wishes that we have. That is the first prayer. This is the first lesson that man has to learn. The other kinds of prayer can only be used as man develops.

In thanking God for all that He has given us, we develop that very thankfulness which man so usually forgets. If we could only reflect upon how many things there are in our life for which we should be thankful and appreciative! But we scarcely ever think about it. We so often think about what we have *not* got, and therefore keep ourselves always unhappy, when we might be thankful to have a few pennies in our purse. Instead of that, we think we should have a few shillings instead! The consequence is that man forgets to develop the thankful nature; he is unthankful to everyone, and therefore, whatever is done for him, he is still unthankful.

It is the same with all the trouble and struggle that there is in the world. It is his neglect of all that is done for him that causes the spread of unthankfulness. Having forgotten the prayer of thanking God, how can he thank man?

How that beautiful custom is disappearing of saying grace before partaking of the meal! This custom is no longer to be found at fashionable tables; only at houses where there is no fashion; for, when fashion comes, the things that are helpful, moral, and spiritual are forgotten. But what a beautiful thought it is to say grace even before a humble dinner! When thanks have been given to God, however simple the dinner may be, it becomes delicious because of the feeling of thankfulness, the feeling that this is a gift that has been bestowed upon us.

When Sa'adi was traveling to Persia, footsore because he had to walk with bare feet in the hot sun, it was so painful to walk that he was thinking; "There can be no one in the world who is so wretched and miserable as I." But two minutes did not pass before he came across a person whose feet were both useless, so that he was crawling along the ground and only progressing with great difficulty. This caused a prayer to rise in Sa'adi's heart, and he became thankful he was not afflicted like that. He thought, "If I have no shoes, at least my feet are healthy and sound."

It is when we are blind to the goodness, kindness, sympathy, service and help which our fellow men give to us, that we become discontented. There is so much to look at in our lives to excite the feeling of thankfulness in us.

Then there is the mystical meaning of thankfulness. That person who is always grudging, is so much the more in need of prayer. If he prays he will prepare influences which will remove the miseries and wretchedness in his mind, for all this misery is created by his mind during the act of grumbling and having a grudge. The person who is thankful and contented, and appreciative of all that befalls him in life, develops the sense of goodness in his life. The more appreciative he is, the more thankful he becomes and the more does he receive. Thankfulness and appreciation inevitably attract more of their like to themselves. All that we give is also given to us. But grumbling and grudging also attract their like to ourselves. If the person to whom we give a reward or gift receives it grudgingly and grumblingly, shall we give him more? And then, the fact that we do not give him more gives him still more to grumble about! But the person who is glad and thankful and appreciative of what is done for him, you think he is so good. It gives you such a feeling and such happiness to see him happy and appreciative and contented that he encourages you to do more, and it encourages others to do good also.

Besides thankfulness, there is the request for forgiveness and mercy. The effects of this are also to be seen in our daily life. A servant or child or young man who is abrupt will push against you and never say, "I am sorry." But another person says, "I am sorry," and at once you have forgotten the harm that he has inadvertently done to you. That is the effect which his request for forgiveness has produced.

In some countries and among some people (as, for instance, in France) there is a custom that when a person meets you at the door or on the stairs he shall take off his hat and say, "Pardon." There is no reason why he should do so except that he chanced to meet you, and he thinks that perhaps he should be forgiven. We find that the sensitiveness of man's heart is so delicate that even the presence of a stranger causes a jar. But by saying, "Pardon," that uncomfortable feeling is at once removed, and, in the place of that, the good feeling of friendship is introduced. However great a fault may be, if this person only comes and says, "I am very sorry; I will never do it again; pray forgive," the friendship at once comes back. On the other hand, however trivial and slight the fault may have been, if pride prevents the man from asking forgiveness and pardon, perhaps he will lose that friendship for the rest of his life. His pride prevents him from asking pardon. The fault may have been very small, and he may say, "I do not care about it," and yet the friendship is broken. How many there are who would be ready to forgive if only the person came and said, "I am sorry." But everybody will not do it; they will not admit they have been in fault.

To ask forgiveness of another produces a proper sense of justice in one's mind. He perceives the need for asking God to pardon his faults. When he asks for forgiveness, that forgiveness develops in his nature too, and he becomes ready to forgive others. Christ says in His prayer, "Forgive us as we forgive others." The virtue, the secret, is in that. By asking forgiveness of God, you give up the desire to demand forgiveness from your fellow man, and you desire to give forgiveness to him. We see this with the Arabs and Bedouins in Mecca and the desert. They are so ready to fight one another and kill each other. They may be fighting, and actually have their knives drawn to kill one another, and yet if a third person comes and says, "Forgive, for the sake of God and the Prophet," as soon as they hear these words they both throw away their knives and shake hands, and the handshake is the seal of friendship. Though the Bedouin has no education, yet he has such a devotion to God and His Prophet that no sooner does he hear these words than he at once offers his hand, and from that day there is no spite nor evil thought in his heart.

If we only had that! With all our education and learning, with all the claims of civilization that we make, we are not as good as these. We retain the bitterness in our hearts. We never reflect what a poison it is. The very person who would shudder at the idea of having something in his body that is decayed and offensive—something that should not be there, but should be taken off or cut out or removed—will tolerate that poison of bitterness in his mind: he will not take it out; he will foster it. Had he not lacked the sense of forgiveness and had he not neglected to cultivate the habit of asking forgiveness, he would have become ready to forgive and forget.

Have you ever experienced the joy when two friends, who have quarreled, have mutually asked forgiveness of one another? It is as if there were no more possibility of ill feeling. It is the most delightful feeling. It feels as if the doors of heaven were open for both. When the bitterness has gone, it is as if a mountain had gone, and the heart were free again.

The third part of the first kind of prayer is our need. This is a delicate thing, and yet it is a great virtue. What a beautiful nature it is that will refrain from asking relief from trouble, from difficulty

PRAYER

and suffering, except from the one Friend. This is a virtue and not pride. The door of faith is kept open for that Friend upon Whom they can call and ask and obtain ease. "There is One to Whom I can go in my trouble and distress and despair. You are the One, the only One. You are He before Whom nothing is hid. If I desire to unburden myself of this trouble, You, O Lord, are He to Whom I will go."

What a great thing this is! What a sense of honor it is that causes him to refrain from telling his suffering to anyone but God, believing that He will help more than anyone can help. Perhaps another man could help, but it will not bring the satisfaction that comes when it is God that has given the help. What a great pleasure, what a great honor God has done to give him help! That is what comes when the problem has been solved which comes into the life of every noble man, everyone with tender feelings, with inherited good and religious sentiments—solved by deciding "There is no one whom I will ask in my poverty and trouble and need, but only God." These are three things that go to make up the first kind of prayer.

There is a story that a king was traveling and hunting in the woods, and the king was hungry and stopped at the house of a peasant, who treated him very kindly. When the king was leaving this peasant, he was so touched with his kindness that, without telling him that he was a king, he said to him, "Take this ring, and if ever you are in trouble, come to me in the city, and I will see what I can do for you." After a time there was a famine, and the peasant was in great trouble, and his wife and child were dying; and he set out to go and see this man. When he showed the ring, he was brought to the king. And when he entered the room, he saw the king busy in prayer; and when the king came near to him, he said, "What were you doing?" "Praying for peace and love and happiness among my subjects," said the king. "So there is one greater than you," said the peasant, "to whom you must go for what you seek? Then I will go to him who is greater and on whom even your destiny depends." He would accept no help; and at last the king had to send what was needed quietly to his home, first saying that no one must tell him that it came from the king.

What honor, what spirit it brings when man fixes his trust on Him Who is called "Almighty," Who is Almighty. Rumi says, "When the fire, air, earth, and water all seem to us dead things, the elements, yet they are servants to God, they work for Him, and they always obey Him!" And he goes on to say, in another part of his *Masnavi*: "Man, when he becomes intelligent, begins to see causes. But it is the superman who sees the Cause of causes, the Source of causes." God is the Cause of causes, the precedent Cause. One who looks at the precedent Cause sees the cause of all in time. A person may study causes all his life, and yet never come to understand the Cause of causes. All causes before that Cause become effects! That Cause remains the Cause which is called "the Word"; then it became Light. "When the Word was spoken," says the Qur'an, "all things came to existence." "Without Him" (the Word), says St. John, "was not anything made that was made."

What is this Cause? It is that inner divine Impulse which has made itself active in every direction, and has accomplished whatever it purposed. It is that which has accomplished all things. The one Cause behind all things is the cause which we call the Power of God.

There are two more ways of prayer.

When people have evolved, they begin to use a still higher prayer. That prayer is the adoration of the immanence of God in the sublimity of Nature. If we read the lives of all the Prophets and Teachers from Krishna to Buddha, Moses to Muhammad, Abraham to Christ, we see how they dwelt in the jungles, and went into the forests, sat beneath trees, and there recognized the divine immanence in all around them. It is a prayer—not to a God in heaven, but to a God living in heaven and on earth—both.

What will praise of God, praise of His creation, praise of His nature, develop in man? It develops in him such an art that nothing can compare with it, a sense of music with which no music can be compared. He begins to see how natures are attracted to one another, and how they harmonize; he sees how inharmonies are produced. The causes of all such things become clear to him, once he begins to see into Nature, to admire the beauty of its construction, its life, its growth, as soon as he begins to study Nature and its causes.

Those who have praised Nature through their art appeal directly to man's heart. Those who praise Nature in their music become artists in music, and those who have expressed their praise in poetry and verse are seen to be great poets. All of them appeal to the heart of man because they have seen God. They have seen Him in Nature, and not alone in Nature, but also on earth. They have turned earth into heaven. That is the next step, the higher step.

Zoroaster has said, "Look at the sun when you pray, at the moon when you pray, at the fire when you pray." People therefore call them sun-worshipers, fire-worshipers, when all the time this worship was merely a way of directing man's attention to all the witnesses of God which express His nature. The one who cannot see any trace of God anywhere, can see Him by looking at all these beautiful things, and observing the harmonious working of all these things.

From beginning to end, the Qur'an points to Nature, showing how by the sun that rises in the morning, and by the moon that appears in the evening, by the Nature that is over all—there is God! Why does the Qur'an always express it this way? If you wish to have some proof of Good, look at Nature and see how wisely it is made—or is it without wisdom? "Mankind, with your wisdom you become so proud that you think there is nothing else worthy. You know not that there is a Perfection of Wisdom before which man is not as a drop to the ocean." Man looks at the surface of the ocean. Yet he is so small that he cannot even be compared to one of its drops, limited as he is in intellect and in knowledge. He seeks to find out the whole creation, whereas those who have touched it, have bowed to God, forgetting their limited selves. After that, God remained, and spoke through them. Such are the only beings who have been able to give any truth to the world.

As Amir says, "He who has lost his limited self, he it is who has attained the High Presence." Do we not forget ourselves when we behold the Vision of Beauty? If we are blind to beauty, we cannot see it, and then we cannot forget ourselves in the beauty and sublimity of the vision.

When we perceive the beauty of Nature, we bow our head in love and admiration. "I cannot study you, for you are too great, you are too beautiful. The only thing left for me to do is to bow my head in prostration at your feet."

If we could only see this perfect beauty around us, if we only had our eyes opened to it, we should at once bow the head in all humility before ever attempting to make a study of it. No pride could find a place in our heart. Without any doubt we should bow our heads before this beauty and wisdom of the Creator, the art of the Creator, and His skill in the flowers, plants and leaves; in the construction of man, his birth, and all other things in life.

It would suffice, did we but once ask how all these things have come—that, as the poet says, "Where there are no teeth, milk is given. When the teeth come, the food suitable for teeth comes also." The eyes are so delicate, and yet a delicate eyelid is formed for them, to cover them and protect them! How all the organs of man's body are fitted and suited for the purpose for which they are made! With all that, there is also the beauty of the art with which the things are made and the height of beauty is attained in the skill shown in the making of mankind.

Whoever has seen beauty, has found that beauty cannot exist without wisdom. Wisdom is behind creation. The one life which has created rocks, trees, plants, animals, birds and all things, is both one life and one wisdom. The flower, the leaf, the fruit and branches, all come from one root, even though they have different names. It is all one. It might be called He or She; yet it is both. When we see that Life with Wisdom is both He and She, we see that Wisdom is behind all things that we see. And then we say that that which is behind all things, is a Person Whom we call God.

The third way of prayer is still greater. It is the way followed by philosophers and mystics. Advancement in this spiritual path is gradual. One cannot use this third way without first having used the other two kinds of prayer.

The third kind of prayer is that of Invocation of the Nature of God, of the Truth of His Being. These are symbolic names. In their meaning there is a subtlety. God's nature is explained in this form of prayer; He is analyzed. The benefit of this prayer is perceived when one has arrived on this plane and the benefit is that he has passed from being a human being—as in the first prayer—through being a holy being, as in the second prayer—to become a God-conscious man. Why? Because this third prayer is in order to bring man still closer to God. Not only does this prayer draw him closer to God, but it makes him forget his limited self until it is entirely forgotten in the end, leaving only the Self of God—the only ideal and aim of all Teachers.

Man has not arrived at his ideal goal until he has used prayer to help him to this stage.

When we look at things from a mystical point of view, we shall find that there is one single straight line, which is called *Aim*. That line represents the line of the life of any being; the upper end is God, the lower end is man. The line is one. Though that line is one to the mystic and the philosopher, in the realization of the Truth, yet the line is unlimited at the upper end, limited at the other. One end is immortality, the other is mortality.

The innermost yearning of life is to see the ends brought together. It is the third prayer that draws the end which is man near to the end which is God. When he invokes the Names of God, man forgets his limitations, and he impresses his soul with the thought of the Unlimited. This brings him to the ideal of Unlimitedness.

This is the secret of life's attainment.

Man is the picture or reflection of his imagination. He is as large as he thinks himself, as great as he thinks himself, as small as he thinks himself. If he thinks he is incapable, he remains incapable; if he thinks himself foolish, he will be foolish, and will remain foolish; if he thinks himself wise, he will be wise, and become wiser every moment; if he thinks himself mighty, he is mighty. Those who have proved themselves to be the greatest warriors, where did their might come from? It was from their thought, their feeling that "I am a mighty one." The idea of "mighty one" was impressed on their soul, and the soul became might. The poet had poetry impressed on his soul, and so the soul became a poet. Whatever is impressed on man's soul, with that the soul becomes endowed, and that the soul will become. If the devil impresses himself on man's soul, he will become a devil; if God impresses Himself on man's soul, he will turn into God!

The God-Ideal

God is Love

God and the God-Ideal may be explained as the sun and the light. As there are times when the sun becomes covered by clouds, so there are times when the God-Ideal becomes covered by materialism. But if the cloud for a moment covers the sun, that does not mean that the sun is lost to you; and so, if in the reign of materialism the God-Ideal seems to have disappeared, yet God is there just the same. The condition of the world is like the ever-rising and falling waves. Sometimes it seems to rise and sometimes to fall, but with every rising and falling wave the sea is the same; and so, with all its changes, life is the same.

We find that during the past few years all over the world there has come a phase when the God-Ideal seems entirely forgotten. It does not mean that churches have disappeared, it does not mean that God does not exist, but that a light that once was there has been covered, has ceased to light us. But at the same time, as there is night after the day, so these changes of condition come in life: light and darkness.

In the age of science on the one side and materialism on the other and commercialism on the top, man seems to have blinded himself in acquiring wealth and power, and sees nothing else. It is not that there is not the search for light (it is the nature of every soul to search for light), but the great question is, how can the light come when nation is against nation, race against race, the followers of one religion against the followers of another; how can there be Peace and how can there come Light? The sign of the day is that all things are clear, and the sign of the night is that nothing can be found or seen; there are clouds. The most dreadful nightmare the world has ever seen has just passed away; and, although that wave, that nightmare, seems to have gone, its effect is still here, and the effect that is left is worse than the cause, for prejudice is worse than bloodshed. When man thirsts for the blood of his fellow man, how can we say that there is light? If a man can eat joyfully at his table when his neighbor is dying of hunger, where is the light? That is the condition of humanity today. And what is the cause? It is because the Light, the God-Ideal, is not there. I was once amused by a very simple answer from a maid when someone came to the door and knocked, and the maid was not free to go at once, but took her time; when at last she came, the man was very angry, and said: "Why did you not open the door quickly?" I asked the maid: "What do you think was the reason for the person's being angry?" And she said, with her innocent expression, "Because there is no God with him."

The word of Christ is that God is Love; and if God is Love, then we, every one of us, can prove God in us by expressing God in our life. Yes, according to the external customs of the different religions, one goes to Church, one to the Mosque, one to the Synagogue, and one to the Temple of Buddha; but the inner Church is neither in the Mosque nor in the Synagogue, but in the heart of man, where God abides and which is the habitation of Christ. With this divine element lighted in man's heart he will go to the House of Prayer, and then his prayer will be heard. There is a well-known story in India of a girl crossing a place where a Muslim was performing his prayers; and the law is that no one should cross where a person is praying. When the girl returned, the man said to her: "How insolent! Do you know what you have done?" "What did I do?" said the girl. And the man said that no one was allowed to cross. "I did not mean any harm," said the girl, "but tell me, what do you mean by praying?" "For me, prayer is thinking of God," said the man. "Oh!" she said, "but I was going to see my young man, and I was thinking of him and I did not see you; and if you were thinking of God, how did you see me?"

The idea, therefore, is that prayer becomes living if it is offered from a living heart; from a dead heart, prayer has no meaning, and is dead. There is a story of an Arab that he was running to the mosque where the Prayer of God was being offered, but before he could arrive the prayers were finished. On his way he met a man coming from the mosque, and asked him: "Are the prayers finished?" The man replied that they were finished, and the other sighed deeply and said, "Alas!" Then the man asked: "Will you give me the virtue of your sigh in exchange for the virtue of my prayers?" And the other agreed. Next day the simple man saw the Prophet in a dream, who told him that he had made a bad bargain, for that one sigh was worth all the prayers of a lifetime, for it was from the heart.

There are different human beings in different stages of evolution, and it is natural that every human being, according to his particular stage of evolution, imagines God before him when he prays. Is it a question for anyone else to judge the one who prays, and to say, "God is not this or that"? Persons who force their beliefs on others often put them against that belief, even if it were the true belief. It requires a great deal of tact, thought, and consideration to explain the belief, or to correct the belief, of another. In the first place, it is insolent on the part of man to wish to explain God, although man today would like, not only to explain, but even to examine whether the spirit of God exists. The other day I was much amused to hear that there are people who not only want to take photographs of the spirits, but even to weigh the soul! It was a good thing in ancient times when the state had respect for the God-Ideal and religion, and taught that respect to humanity. Today man wishes to use what he calls "freedom" in religion, even in the foundation of all religions, the God-Ideal! But it must be remembered that it is not the path of freedom that leads to the goal of freedom, but the path of the God-Ideal that leads to the goal of Truth.

Man has a respect for mother or father, husband or wife, or for superiors, but they have limited personalities; where then shall he give most respect? Only to one being—to God. Man can love another human being, but by the very fact of his loving another human being he has no scope; to express all the love that is there, he must love the unlimited God. One admires all that is beautiful, in color, tone, or form; but all that is beautiful has its limitations; when one rises above limitations, there is that perfection which is God alone. Many people say, "Yes, the perfection of all things, of love, harmony, and beauty, is God; but where is the personality of God?" It is this difficulty which some feel when at a loss to find something to adore or worship different from all they see. In all ages men have, perhaps, worshiped idols, or the sun, or fire, or some other form as God, because they were not able to see farther than their eyes could see. Of course, it is easy to criticize anyone or to look at anyone with contempt, but really that shows that every soul has a desire for someone to admire, to adore, and to worship.

Although there can be no trace of the personality of God to be found on the surface, yet one can see that there is a source from which all personality comes, and a goal to which all must return. And if there is one source, what a great Personality that one Source must be! It cannot be learnt by great intellect, or not even by the study of metaphysics or comparative religion, but only understood by a pure and innocent heart full of love.

The great personalities who have descended on earth from time to time to awaken in man that love which is his divine inheritance found an echo in innocent souls rather than in great intellects. Man often confuses wisdom with cleverness and cleverness with wisdom. But these two are different; man can be wise and can be clever, and man can be clever and not wise; and by cleverness a person will strive and strive, and will not reach God. It is a stream—the stream of love—which leads towards God.

Two Points of View

There are two points of view from which one sees the God-Ideal. One is the point of view of the imaginative, and the other the point of view of the God-conscious. The former is the point of view of the minor soul, and the latter is that of the soul which is major. For the one thinks that there is a God, and the other sees God. The believer who adorns his God with all that the imagination can supply, sees God as all beauty, as all goodness, and as the most merciful and compassionate God, and recognizes Him as the Almighty, the Supreme Being. He sees in God the true Judge, and he expects one day to receive justice from Him. He knows that in God he will find at last the perfect love on which he can rely entirely. He sees in God the Friend to Whom he can turn in sorrow and in joy. He calls Him his Father and his Lord, his Father and Mother; and all that is good and beautiful he recognizes as coming from God. Really speaking, he makes an intelligible form of God, that being the only condition by which he can see God. And the believer who has imagined God as high as his imagination will allow him to, he adores Him, asks His forgiveness, looks for His help, and hopes one day to attain to Him, and he feels that there is Someone nearer to him than anyone else in life, Whose mercy is always with him.

It is this point of view that is called monotheism—believing in the personality of God, a Personality which man makes to the best of his ability. Therefore the God of the monotheist is within him, made by his mind. But it is the form of God that he makes. The spirit is always the same, hidden behind the form that man has made because he needs a form. No doubt at this stage the God of the believer is the form made by Him, the form of a human being. God is behind that form, and He answers His worshiper through that form. Someone once said to a Brahman, "O ignorant man, you have worshiped this idol for years. Do you think that it can ever answer you?" "Yes," said the Brahmin, "even from this idol of stone the answer will come if the faith is real. But if you have not real faith, you will have no answer even from the God in Heaven." Man, who knows and sees all things by his senses and his feelings, and who tries to picture everything by his imagination—things that he has neither seen nor known, such as spirits, angels, fairies—it is natural that he should make God intelligible to himself by means of his imagination.

The other point of view, which I have called the major point of view, is perhaps less interesting to some and more interesting to others; for this is the true point of view. When a person begins to see all goodness as being the goodness of God, all the beauty that surrounds him as the divine beauty, he no doubt begins to worship a visible God, and no doubt, as his heart constantly loves and admires the divine beauty in all that he sees, he begins to see in all that is visible one single vision; all becomes for him a single vision—the vision of the Beauty of God. His love for beauty increases his capacity to such a degree that great virtues, such as tolerance and forgiveness, spring naturally from his heart. Even things that mostly people look upon with contempt, he views with tolerance. The brotherhood of humanity he does not need to learn, for he does not see humanity, he sees only God. And as this vision develops, it becomes a divine vision that occupies every moment of his life. In nature he sees God, and in man he sees His image, and in art and poetry he sees the dance of God. The waves of the sea bring him the message from above, and the swaying of the branches in the breeze seems to him a prayer. For him there is a constant contact with his God. He knows neither horror nor terror, nor any fear. Birth and death are to him only little changes in life. Life is for him a moving picture which he loves and admires, and yet he is free from all. He is one among all the world. He himself is happy, and he makes others happy. This point of view is the pantheistic point of view.

In reality, these two points of view are the natural consequences of human evolution, and really one cannot separate them. No one reaches old age without having passed through youth, and no one attains to the pantheistic point of view without having held the monotheistic. And if anyone arrives at the pantheistic point of view at once, without holding the monotheistic, it would be like a person becoming a man without having been a child, which is void of beauty.

There are, certainly, two possibilities of error. One is that made by the monotheist when he continues to adore the God he has made, without allowing himself to see the point of view of the pantheist. In order to love God, he limits his own God, which does not mean that God is really limited, but He is limited for that person. The ways of childhood are charming in a child, but a grown-up person with the characteristics of a child is absurd. When man begins his belief in God by monotheism, it is the best way, but when he ends his life without having made any progress, he has lost in his life the greatest opportunity. The man who makes this mistake separates man from God, who, in reality, cannot be divided. For God and man are as the two ends of one line. When a believer in God conceives of God as a separate entity and man a being separate from Him, he makes himself an exile—an exile from the Kingdom of God. He holds fast the form of God created by himself, and he does not reach the Spirit of God. However good and virtuous he has been in life, however religious in his actions, he has not fulfilled the purpose of his life.

A mistake is made by the pantheist when he holds the idea that all which he can conceive of and all that answers to his five senses, he believes alone exists. For by this mistake he holds to the form of God and loses His Spirit. All that we can comprehend in man is not all there is to be comprehended. There is something which is beyond all our comprehension. And if the depths of man are too far to be touched by man, how can he hope to touch the depths of God? All that is visible is in reality one body, a body that may be called the Body of God; but behind, there is the Spirit of God. What is behind this Body is the Source and Goal of all beings. And, of course, the part which is the spirit is the most important part. The pantheist who recognizes the divinity only of that which is comprehensible to him, although pantheism may be to him a great ideal, is yet one groping in the dark. All that is subject to change, all that is not constant, all that passes through birth and death, may also some day be destroyed. The man who limits the Divine Being to something that is subject to destruction, the man who cannot feel the trace of the Divine Being in something that is beyond his comprehension, that man is astray. True pantheism is: God is all, and all is God, the known and the unknown; all that exists within and without; God is all that exists, and nothing exists save He.

The beginning of monotheism may be called deism, a belief in Someone higher than oneself. And for the souls who have reached this stage of evolution, for these souls many lessons have been given by the Sages. The Sages have taught them to adore the sun, fire, water, certain trees, and many idols. And no doubt, behind all these teachings there is always the wisdom of the Masters. The lessons given to certain peoples were not for others, as what is suitable for one period is not suitable for another. And for teaching pantheism there were also elementary lessons, such as the idea of many gods, as among the ancient Greeks and the ancient Hindus and the old Egyptians. All these peoples believed in many gods, and this lesson was given to them to see in different things the same Spirit of God. Every god had as his characteristics certain human traits, and by this means man was taught to become capable of recognizing God in his fellow man, to become tolerant and forgiving; also he was led to concentrate and meditate on certain human characteristics, considering them as something divine. Consideration and respect for humanity was taught by meditation on certain traits.

Man without knowledge of these two different points of view, and strongly impressed by materialistic ideas, often looks upon God as a force or an energy, but he denies forcibly that God can have a personality. No doubt it would be a great mistake to call God a personality, but it is a still greater mistake when man denies the Personality of God. And if you ask this person: "What is your source? What is your goal? Are you yourself a personality? Is it possible that you should be a personality yourself when the Goal and the Source from which you come is not a Personality?," he has no answer. It is the seed, which is the origin of the flower and the fruit, that is also the result of the flower and the fruit. Therefore man is the miniature of the Personality of God; God is the seed from which comes the personality. Man, in the flowering of his personality, expresses the Personality of God. It is a subject that cannot be discussed because one is able to distinguish all things by comparison, and, because God is the Only Being, He cannot be compared, and even to use the word *personality* in speaking of God would be a mistake. There cannot be a better way of looking at the God-Ideal than to consider Him as being *perfection* in the widest and fullest meaning of the word.

The Kingship of God

The God-Ideal has been regarded by different men differently. Some have idealized God as the King of Earth and Heaven, some have a conception of God as a Person, others think of God as an abstraction; some believe in God, others do not, some raise the ideal of the Deity to the highest heaven, others bring it down to the lowest depth of earth; some picture God in Paradise, others make an idol and worship it. There are many ideas and many beliefs, different names, such as pantheism, idolatry, belief in a formless God, or belief in many gods and goddesses, but all are striving after something in one way or another. If I were asked how many conceptions there are of God, I would say, "As many as there are souls"; for all, whether wise or foolish, have some conception of God. Everyone knows God in some way and has his own picture of Him, either as a Man, as the Absolute, as Goodness, as Something beautiful or illuminating; everyone has some conception; and for the one who does not believe in God, even for him the Name exists. Very often the unbeliever is an unbeliever because of his own vanity, though this is not always so. He says that only simple people believe in God; he sees that there are millions of simple souls who worship God, and yet it does not raise them higher, and so he sees no virtue in the worship of God. Others believe in the God-Ideal so long as they are happy, but when their condition changes, when sorrow and trouble come, they begin to doubt whether there really is a God. I have often met people who had had a great belief in God, but having lost a dear one, and having vainly prayed and implored God that they might keep him, they had lost their belief. I once met a most unhappy mother who had given up her belief in God after the death of her only child. It grieved me to think that a soul so religious, tender, and fine, by that one great sorrow in life, had given up her faith; I told her that while I sympathized with her most deeply, at the same time, in giving up her faith she had brought to herself a much greater loss—a loss for which nothing could make up.

In the Bible we read, and in the other scriptures, that we should glorify the Name of God. There is a question: Is God raised higher by man's worshiping Him; or is He made greater by man's belief in Him? The answer is that God is independent of all that man can do for Him. If man worships God, believes in Him, and glorifies Him, it is for man's own good; for belief in God serves the greatest and only purpose in life, for the fulfillment of which man was born, and that purpose is the attainment of that perfection which may be called divine.

Why must God be called a King? Why not any other name? The answer is that it is impossible for words to explain or define God, but all that man can do is to use the best word for the Greatest Being, the Supreme Being; and he uses this word because language is poor, and he can find no other or better one.

Again comes the question of the metaphysician or the philosopher, when he reads: *All is God and God is all.* He says: "If God is goodness, what, then, is the opposite of goodness? Is it outside God? If so, God is limited. Then something else exists as well as God. Are there two powers, rival powers? What is the power called

evil?" It is true that God is all, but you would not call a man's
shadow the man. What is evil, then? It is only a shadow. What is
illness? It is another illusion. In reality, there is only life, real existence; illness is lack of life; it is a shadow, an illusion. The Being of
God is recognized by His attributes. Therefore, man speaks of God
as the just God; he sees all power, all goodness, in God; but when
the situation is changed, when he sees God as injustice, he begins
to think that God is powerless, and to judge the action of God. But
one must look at this from a different point of view. Human beings
are limited, imperfect, and from our own imperfect standpoint we
try to judge the Perfect Being, or His perfect action. In order to
judge, our vision must become as wide as the universe; then we
might have a little glimpse of the Justice which is perfect in itself.
But when we try to judge every action by limiting God and by
attaching the responsibility of every action to God, we confuse our
faith, and by our own fault we begin to disbelieve. The error is in
man's nature; from childhood we think all we do and say is just
and fair, and so when man thinks of God he has his own conception, and by that he tries to judge God and His justice; if he is
forgiving, he tries to overlook God's apparent injustice, and to find
goodness in God and to see the limitation of man. This is better,
but in the end man will realize that every movement is controlled
and directed from One Source, and that Source is the Perfection of
Love, Justice, and Wisdom, a Source where nothing lacks. But it is
so difficult for man to have a perfect conception of the God-Ideal,
and he cannot begin in a first lesson to conceive of God as perfect.
So the wise must be tolerant of all the forms in which souls picture
their God.

There is a story told of Moses. One day he was passing through
a farm, and he saw a peasant boy sitting quietly and speaking to
himself, saying: "O God, I love You so; if I saw You here in these
fields I would bring You soft bedding and delicious dishes to eat, I

would take care that no wild animals could come near You. You are so dear to me, and I so long to see You; if You only knew how I love You I am sure You would appear to me." Moses heard, and said: "Young man, how can you dare to speak of God so? He is the Formless God, and no wild beast nor bird could injure Him who guards and protects all." The young man bent his head sorrowfully and wept. Something was lost for him, and he felt most unhappy. And then revelation came to Moses as a Voice from within, which said: "Moses, what have you done? You have separated a sincere lover from Me. What does it matter what I am called or how I am spoken to? Am I not in all forms?" This story throws a great light, and teaches that it is only the ignorant who accuse another of a wrong conception of God.

This teaches us how gentle we ought to be with the faith of another; as long as he has the spark of the love of God, this spark should be slowly blown upon that the flame may rise; if not, that spark will be extinguished. How much the spiritual development of mankind in general depends upon a religious man! He can either spread the light, or diminish it by forcing his belief on others.

Everyone thinks the other person must believe in and worship his God. Everyone has his own conception of God, and this conception makes the steppingstone to the true Ideal of God. Then there are others who believe in God, but do not show their belief in any outward religious tendency. People often misunderstand them, and yet there is something very beautiful hidden in their heart, not understood, not known. There is a story told in the East of a man who used to avoid going to the house of prayer, who showed no outward sign, so that his wife often wondered if he had any belief in God; she thought a great deal about this, and was very anxious about it. One day she said to her husband: "I am very happy today." The man was surprised, and asked what made her happy, and she said: "I was under a false impression, but now that I have found

out the truth, I am glad." He asked: "What has made you glad?"
And she replied: "I heard you saying the Name of God in your
sleep." He said: "I am very sorry." It was too precious, too great for
him to speak of, and he felt it was a great blow, after having hidden
this secret in the deepest part of his being because it was too sacred
to speak of. He could not bear it, and he died. We cannot say from
the outward appearance who believes and who does not believe.
One person may be pious and orthodox and it may mean nothing;
another may have a profound love for the Deity, and a great
knowledge of Him, and no one may know it.

What benefit does man receive from believing in the Kingship
of God? How does he derive real help from his belief? He must
begin by realizing the nobility of human nature. Not that one must
expect everything to be good and beautiful, and, if one's expecta-
tion is not realized, then there is no hope of progress; for man is
limited, his goodness is limited. No one has ever proved to be your
ideal; you may make an ideal of your imagination, and, whenever
you see goodness to be lacking, you may give it from your own
heart and so complete the nobility of human nature. This is done
by patience, tolerance, kindness, forgiveness. The lover of goodness
loves every little sign of goodness. He overlooks the faults and fills
up the gaps by pouring out love and filling up that which is lacking.
This is real nobility of soul. Religion, prayer, worship, are all
intended to ennoble the soul, not to make it narrow, sectarian,
bigoted. One cannot arrive at true nobility of spirit if one is not
prepared to forgive imperfect human nature. For all, worthy or
unworthy, require forgiveness, and only in this way can one rise
above the lack of harmony and beauty, until at last one arrives at
the stage when one reflects what one has collected.

All the riches of love, kindness, tolerance, and good manners
a man then reflects, and he throws the light onto the other person

and brings out those virtues in that other, just as watering a plant makes the leaves and buds open and the flowers blossom. This brings one nearer to the Perfection of God, in Whom alone one sees all that is perfect, all that is divine. As it is said in the Bible: "Be ye perfect, even as your Father in Heaven is perfect."

Belief in God

It is the spirit of all souls which is personified in all ages as God. There are periods when this spirit is materialized in the faith of humanity and worshiped as God, the Sovereign and the Lord of both worlds, as Judge, Sustainer, and Forgiver; but there are periods when this realization has become less in humanity, when mankind has become absorbed in the life of the world more than in the spiritual ideal. Therefore the belief in God comes to humanity like tides in the sea. Every now and then it appears on the surface, mostly with a Divine Message given as an answer to the cry of humanity at a certain period. So, in the life of individuals, at times the belief in God comes as tides in the sea, with an impulse to worship, to serve God, to search for God, to love God, and to long for God-communication. The more the material life of the world is before one's eyes, the more the spiritual impulse is closed. The spiritual impulse therefore rises especially at times of sorrow and of disappointment through life.

The belief in God is natural, but in life both art and nature are necessary. So God, Who exists independent of our making Him, must be made by us for our own comprehension. To make God intelligible, first man must make his own God. It is on this principle that the idea of many gods and the custom of idol-worship were based in the ancient religions of the world. God cannot be two. The God of each is the God of all, but in order to comprehend that God we each have to make our own God. Some of us seek for justice; we can seek for God, Who is just. Some of us look for beauty; we must find it in the God of beauty. Some of us seek for love; we must find it in the God of mercy and compassion. Some of us wish for strength and power; we must find it in God Almighty. The seeking of every soul in this world is different, distinct, and peculiar to himself, and he can best attain to it by finding the object of his search in God.

The moment one arrives at this belief, no question need he ask of his fellow man, for the answer to every question that springs from his mind he finds in his own heart. The dwelling place of God, which is called heaven, is then found in his own heart. The Friend on Whom one can constantly depend, Someone Whom one can always trust; Someone Whose sympathy and love is secure; Someone Who will never fail, whatever happens; Someone Who is strong enough to help; Someone Who is sufficiently wise to guide in life, he will find in his own heart.

Those who, out of their materialistic view, cannot believe in the God-Ideal, lose a great deal in their lives. That ideal which is the highest and best ideal, the only ideal worth loving, worth worshiping, worth longing for, worth the sacrifice of all one has, and worth depending upon during the daylight and through the darkness of night, is God; and he who has God in his life, has all he needs; he who has not God, he, having all things of this mortal world, is lonely; he is in the wilderness even if he be in the midst of the crowd. The journey of the Sufi, therefore, is to God. It is Divine Knowledge which he seeks; it is the realization of God-consciousness which is his goal.

The Existence of God

The existence of God is a question which arises in every mind, whether in the mind of the believer in God or in the mind of the unbeliever. There are moments when the greatest believer in God questions His existence—whether there really is a God? He finds it, at the second thought, sacrilegious to have a notion such as this, and he tries to get rid of it. But often the question rises in the heart of the unbeliever if it is really true; if there is such a thing as God? The idea of God is inborn in man. The God-Ideal is the flower of the human race; and this flower blooms in the realization of God.

As everything in the objective world has its tendency to rise upwards, so the tendency of the soul can be seen in human aspiration, which always soars upwards, whatever be the sphere of man's consciousness. The man who is only conscious of the material life, his aspirations reach as far as they can reach in material gains, yet he proceeds higher and higher, and remains discontented with all that he achieves through life, owing to the immensity of life in every phase. This craving for the attainment of what is unattainable, gives the soul a longing to reach life's utmost heights. It is the nature of the soul to try and discover what is behind the veil; it is the soul's constant longing to climb heights which are beyond his power; it is the desire of the soul to see something that it has never seen; it is the constant longing of the soul to know something it has never known. But the most wonderful thing about it is that the soul already knows there is something behind this veil, the veil of perplexity; that there is something to be sought for in the highest spheres of life; that there is some beauty to be seen; that there is Someone to be known who is knowable. This desire, this longing, is not acquired; this desire is a dim knowledge of the soul which it has in itself.

Therefore disbelief in the God-Ideal is nothing but a condition which is brought about by the vapours arising from the material life of illusion, and covering as clouds the light of the soul, which is its life. It is therefore that the unbeliever is not satisfied with his unbelief. Yes, sometimes his vanity is fed by it, to think that he is wise in not believing in Someone Whose existence is believed in by numberless blind beings. So he begins to think: "After all, to believe in God is not difficult; any simpleton can believe in the God-Ideal." He takes, therefore, the opposite direction of refusing to believe. He is honest, and yet he is like someone who stands before a wall which hinders his path to progress.

If this world offered to one person all it possesses, even then the soul would not be satisfied because its satisfaction is in its higher aspiration, and it is this higher aspiration which leads to God. The question: "Has man an aspiration because it is his nature, but in the end of the journey he may perhaps not find anything?" may be answered: "There is no question which has no answer, and there is no desire the object of which is lacking." There is appetite, and there is food; there is thirst, and there is water; there is sight, and there is something to be seen. *So there is aspiration, and there is God.* Man knows not what is not. There is no such thing which one knows and which does not exist. For one cannot know what does not exist; something must exist first to enable one to know it.

But there is a question: "Everyone does not know God; does he not then only believe in some idea?" The answer is: "What is the idea? The idea is that out of which all is born. Science, art, music, poetry, religion and nationality, all is born of the idea. If the idea is the source from which all comes, then why is the idea something insignificant, and why is God, Who is the Source and Goal of all, not found in the idea?"

The seeking for God is a natural outcome of the maturity of the soul. There is a time in life when a passion is awakened in the soul which gives the soul a longing for the unattainable, and if the soul does not take that direction, then it certainly misses something in life for which is its innate longing and in which lies its ultimate satisfaction.

Conceptions of God

There are different conceptions of God existing in various periods and known to different people. The people in all ages, seeking for the Deity, have pictured Him in some form or other. It is natural with man. If he is told about someone he has never seen or known, he makes a conception of that person, and he holds his conception as his knowledge of that person until he sees him. There are some who make a conception in their mind of a person whom they have not seen almost as real as the person. The human heart is an accommodation which conceives the idea of God and pictures Him according to man's own mentality. The Buddha of China has Chinese features, and that of Japan has the eyes of Japan; the Buddha of India has the Indian likeness. Man cannot conceive of an angel being any different from a human being, except that he attaches two wings to the angel in order to make it a little different. If the angel were not pictured as man, it would not be an attraction to a human being; therefore, it is natural that in every period people have conceived of the Personality of God as a human personality. No better conception could they have given, for there is nothing in the world which is a more finished personality than the human personality.

People have called God *He*, recognizing the might and power of the Deity. People have called God *She*, recognizing in the Deity

the Mother-principle and beauty. It is the differences of conception
from which have come the many gods and goddesses. It is true,
too, that as many conceptions there are, so many gods are there.
And yet many gods mean many conceptions of the One Only God.
By ignorance of this truth many have fought over their different
gods; and yet the wise man in every period of the world has understood God to be the One and Only Being. For the ordinary mind,
to feel the existence of someone in the idea is not sufficient. It is
too vague. He wishes to feel the existence of someone with his own
hands; then only he can acknowledge something to be existent. The
wise, therefore, have given different objects to such mentalities,
and pointed them out to the people as gods. Some said: "See God
in the sun"; and the person understood. He was not satisfied to
think that God was in the idea; he was much more pleased to know
now that God is seen by him, and God is incomparable even as the
sun, and that God is not reachable. Some wise men have said: "He
is in the fire." Some said, to a simple man who asked to see God:
"Go in the forest and find out a certain tree, and that tree is God."
The search for that tree gave something for that man to do, which
was the first essential thing. And the patience with which he sought
the tree also, did something in his soul. The joy of finding a rare
tree was also a pleasure. And in the end he found, for God is everywhere. Some have made images of different ideas, such as love,
justice, knowledge and power, and called them different goddesses,
molded them into different images, and have given them to man to
worship. Some wise men have said the cow is sacred. Certainly it is
sacred for a farmer whose farming depends upon the cow. His life's
sustenance comes, in every form, from the cow; it is sacred.

The wise have pointed out different objects to man which will
attract man's attention and become objects of concentration for
him to still his mind; for in the mind which is still, God manifests.

Then, again, the wise have presented the God-Ideal to the people in the form of symbols. To simple beings a symbol was God; and to awakened minds the same symbol of God was a revealing factor of the secret of the Deity. If one could only see how marvelously, in the diversity of the conception of the Divine Ideal, wisdom has played its part, guiding the souls of all grades of evolution towards the same goal, which in the end becomes spiritual attainment!

Many Gods

The conception of many gods has come from two sources. One was the idea of the wise to make every kind of power and attribute in a form of deity, and to call it a certain god. It was done in order to give the ordinary mind the most needed thought, that God is in everything and God is all power. Many afterwards misunderstood the idea, and the wisdom behind it became obscured, therefore some wise men had to fight against the ideas of the other wise men. Yet they did not fight with the idea; they fought with the misconception of it. But now, at the present time, when there exists no such idea in Europe of many gods, many have lost their faith after the recent war, saying: "If God is all goodness, all justice, all power, why has such a dreadful thing as war been allowed to take place?" If the same people were accustomed to see, among their many gods, as the Hindus have worshiped for generations, Kali, the goddess of war, it would not have been a new thing for them to know that, if all is from God, not only peace, but even war is from God.

The mystics of all ages have therefore given God many names. The Sufi schools of esotericism have possessed their different names of God, with their nature and secret, and have used them in different meditations along the path of spiritual attainment. Therefore the Sufis have not many gods, but many Names of God, each expressive of a certain attribute. Suppose these Names which the Sufis have used, were not the Names of God—if they had only held in thought words such as mercy, compassion, patience—it would have been a merit, not a person. Merit is not creative, and merit is only something which is possessed. Therefore the attribute is not important; the important one is the possessor of the attribute. Therefore, instead of thinking of success, the Sufi calls upon the God of success. For him the God of success is not a different God; there is only one God, but only by calling upon that Name of God which is expressive of success, he attaches his soul to that perfect Spirit of success.

The other source whence the idea of many gods has come, are the deep thinkers and philosophers, who have seen God in every soul, and every soul making a God of its own, according to its stage of evolution. Therefore there is a saying among the Hindus: "There are as many gods as there are strains of music." In other words, there are numerous imaginations and numberless gods. If ever this idea was taught to the people, it was to break that ignorance of some people who made God confined to heaven, and kept the earth free from His divine Presence: they waited for death to come, when they might be taken into the Presence of God, Who was sitting on the throne of justice in the hereafter. By it they tried to show to the people that God is in every soul, and so, as many souls, so many gods: some advanced, some not advanced, some further advanced, and yet all gods. If there is a struggle, it is a conflict between gods; if there is harmony, it is a friendship between gods. By these terms they wished to make man realize the most essential truth that God is all. No doubt those who misunderstand will always misunderstand.

This idea brought about corruption also, and made people, who regard many gods, interested in the legends of the past which narrated the wars and battles that took place among gods. There-fore the wise had again to come to their rescue, and teach them again of the one God, that by this teaching they might again come to the realization of the oneness of life, which is best realized in the God-Ideal.

The Personality of God

Very often, many who are ready to accept the God-Ideal, question the personality of God. Some say: "If all is God, then God is not a person, for 'all' is not a person: 'all' is what is expressed by the word *all*." This question can be answered that, though the seed does not show the flower in it, yet the seed culminates in a flower, and therefore the flower has already existed in the seed. If one were to say that in the image of the seed the flower was made, it would not be wrong, for the only image of the seed is the flower. If God has no personality, how can we human beings have a personality, who come from Him, out of His own Being, and we who can express the divine in the perfection of our souls? If the bubble is water, certainly the sea is water. How can the bubble be water and the sea not be water? Only the difference between the human personality and the Divine Personality, God's Personality, is that the human personality can be compared; God's Personality has no comparison. Human personality can be compared because of its opposite; God has no opposite, so His Personality cannot be compared. To call God all is like saying God is a number of objects, all of which exist somewhere together. The word *all* does not give that meaning which can explain the God-Ideal; the proper expression for God is *The Only Being.*

The God-Ideal is so enormous that man can never comprehend it fully; therefore the best method which the wise have
adopted is to allow every man to make his own God. By this he
only makes a conception which he is capable of making. He makes
Him the King of the Heavens and of the earth; he makes Him
Judge, greater than all judges; he makes Him Almighty, Who has all
power; he makes Him the Possessor of all grace and glory; he makes
Him the beloved God, merciful and compassionate; he recognizes
in Him the providence, the support, the protection; and he recognizes in Him all perfection. This ideal becomes as a steppingstone
to the higher knowledge of God. The man who has no imagination
to make a God, and the one who is not open to the picture of God
that the other man presents to him, he remains without one, for he
finds no steppingstone to reach that knowledge which his soul
longs for but his doubts deny.

Many would ask if it would not be deceiving oneself to make a
God of one's imagination, Someone Who is not seen in the objective
world. The answer is that our whole life is based and constructed
upon imagination, and if there is one thing in this objective world
which is lasting, it is imagination. The one incapable, who has no
value for imagination, is void of art and poetry, of music, manners,
and culture. He can very well be compared to a rock, which never
troubles to imagine.

Man is not capable of picturing God as other than a person—
a person with all the best qualities, the ideal person. This does not
mean that all that is ugly and evil does not belong to the universe
of God, or, in other words, is not in God Himself. But the water of
the ocean is ever pure, in spite of all the things that may be thrown
into it. The Pure One consumes all impurities, and turns, them all
into purity. Evil and ugliness are only in man's limited conception;
in God's great Being these have no existence; therefore, he is not

wrong who makes God, in his imagination, the God of all beauty, free from ugliness; the God of all the best qualities, free from all evil, for by that imagination he is drawn nearer and nearer every moment of his life to that Divine Ideal which is the seeking of his soul. And, once he has touched divine Perfection, in it he will find the fulfillment of his life.

The Realization of God

In the terms of the Sufis the Self of God is called *Zat*, and His qualities, His merits, are named *Sifat*. The Hindus call the former aspect of God *Purusha* and the latter *Prakriti*, which can be rendered in English by the words *spirit* and *nature*. *Zat*, the Spirit of God, is incomprehensible. The reason is that, That which comprehends Itself is Intelligence, God's real Being; so comprehension has nothing to comprehend in its own Being. No doubt, in our usual terms it is the comprehending faculty in us which we call comprehension; but in this it is not meant so, for intelligence is not necessarily intellect. Merit is something which is comprehensible; it is something which is clear and distinct, so that it can be made intelligible. But intelligence is not intelligible except to its own self. Intelligence knows that *I am*; but it does not know *what I am*. Such is the Nature of God. Intelligence would not have known its own power and existence, if it had not known something besides itself. So God knows Himself by manifestation. Manifestation is the self of God, but a self which is limited, a self that makes Him know that He is perfect when He compares His own Being with this limited self which we call nature. Therefore the purpose of the whole Creation is the realization that God Himself gains by discovering His own Perfection through this manifestation.

Then the idea that has existed in Christianity is also a riddle to solve that we may find out the truth of life. It is the idea of the Trinity. What keeps the soul in perplexity is the threefold aspect of manifestation. As long as the soul remains in this puzzle, it cannot arrive at the knowledge of the One. These three aspects are: the Seer, Sight, and the Seen; the Knower, Knowledge, and the Known. Plainly explained, I would say: these are three aspects of life. One aspect is the person who sees; the other aspect is the sight, or the eyes, by the help of which he sees; and the third aspect is that which he sees. One, therefore, cannot readily accept the idea that, "What I see is the same as myself"; nor can he believe for a moment that, "The medium, by which I see, is myself"; for the three above said aspects seem to be standing separate and looking at one another's face, as the first person, second person, and third person of Brahma. When this riddle is solved by knowing that the three are one, then the purpose of the God-Ideal is fulfilled. For the three veils which cover the One are lifted up. Then they remain no longer three; then there is One, the Only Being. As Hegel says, "If you believe in one God, you are right; if you believe in two Gods, that is true; but if you believe in three Gods, that is right also; for the nature of unity is realized by variety."

Creator, Sustainer, Judge, Forgiver

Why is God called the *Creator*? Because the creation itself is the evidence of some wisdom working. No mechanical creation could result in such perfection as is Nature. All the machines of the scientists are built on the model of Nature's mechanism, and every inspiration that the artist has he receives from Nature. Nature is so perfect in itself that in reality it needs no scientific or artistic improvement upon it, except that, to satisfy the limited human fancies, man develops science and art. And yet it is still the creation of God expressed in art and science through man; as in man God is not absent, but more able in some ways to finish His creation, which necessitates His finishing it as man. No better evidence is needed for a sincere inquirer into the Creator-God. If he only concentrates his mind upon Nature, he certainly must sooner or later have an insight into the perfect wisdom which is hidden behind it. The soul that comes into the world is only a divine ray. The impressions it gets on its way while coming to the earth also are from God. No movement is possible without the command of God; therefore, in all creation, in its every aspect, in the end of search and examination God alone proves to be the only Creator.

The word *Sustainer* is attached to His Name. Jesus Christ said, "Consider the lilies of the field. They toil not, neither do they spin; yet even Solomon in all his glory was not arrayed as one of these." And Rumi explains it further in the *Masnavi*: "Even the spider is not neglected by God, but is supplied with its food." If the smallest germ and worm, insignificant as it is, had depended for its supply upon man, who cannot even always supply himself, how would the creation have gone on? It seems that the creatures who do not worry for their supply, to their mouth their food is conveyed. Man's struggle, it seems, for his supply is greater than that of all other living beings in the lower creation. But what makes it so? It is not God, it is man himself, who is selfish, and who is unfair to his brother, absorbed in his own interests in life. In spite of all famines, the world still has sufficient supplies; but imagine the amount of food that has been sunk in the sea, and how many years the earth, in which man's food is prepared, was neglected by men busy killing one another! If the result of this causes hunger and greater strife, is God to be blamed? It is man who deserves all blame. Sa'adi very subtly explains human nature in regard to providence: it is the most beautiful expression: "The Creator is always busy preparing for me the supply, but my anxiety for my supply is my natural illness." Life is such a phenomenon, if only we dive deep into it, that we find no question is without an answer. It never is so that we need something and are not provided with it. The only difference is between what we think we need and what we really need. The supply is always greater than our need, therefore providence is always a phenomenon. Sometimes we look at it with smiles, at other times with tears. But it is something real and living; and more real it will prove to be if we look at it by climbing to the top of our reason.

God as *Judge* is spoken of by many prophets, and the man of reason and logic has tried to attribute justice to the law. But justice is not law; justice is above the law. Very often, to our limited view, things in the world appear unjust; and often it seems that there is man's law: what he wishes, he does, if he has the power to do it. But behind this illusive appearance there certainly is a strict justice and a real law. No sooner does the heart becoming living than this law manifests. One cannot but marvel at life and nature, to see how great is the justice of God: that it is, to give with the right hand and take with the left—all you give and all you take. No soul has to wait for days or weeks or years, or for death to come, for the law to manifest. Every day is a Judgment Day, and every hour is the hour of justice. A criminal will escape from the prison bars, but he cannot go from under the sky! There is the Judge within and without. When his eyes are closed he is being judged within; when they are open he is being judged without. We are always in a court of justice. If we do not realize it, it is because we are intoxicated by life, and we become like a drunken man in the court, who does not see the judge nor justice.

But what we can marvel most at in life, is to know that, in spite of His great Justice, God is the *Forgiver*. He forgives even more than He judges, for justice comes from His Intelligence, but forgiveness comes from His Divine Love. When His Divine Love rises as a wave, it washes away the sins of a whole life in a moment. For law has no power to stand before love; the stream of love sweeps it away. When before Christ the woman was brought who was accused by everyone of her crime, what arose from the heart of the Master? The law? No; it was love, in the form of mercy and compassion. Even the thought of the Love of God fills the heart with joy, and makes it lightened of its burden. And if, as the religious have always taught, once in a person's life he has asked whole-heartedly for forgiveness, in spite of his whole life's sins he will certainly be forgiven.

The Only King

God is called *King of Heaven and of the earth, and of the seen and unseen beings,* only because we have no better words than the words we use for all the things of this world. To call God *King* does not raise Him in any way higher than the position He has; it only helps us to make His power and glory more intelligible to our mind. And yet there are certain characters which are kingly characters; such characters may be seen in God in their perfection. It does not mean that every person has not that character. It only means that from a higher position a soul shows out that character more, perhaps, than in an ordinary capacity. That character is love hidden behind indifference. In Sufic terms this character is denoted by a Persian word, *Binayaz,* which means "hidden." It does not mean "the hidden God"; it means "hidden beauty." Love expressed is one thing, and love hidden is another thing. Under the veil of indifference love is often hidden, and the Sufi poets have pictured it most beautifully in their verses, which are nothing but pictures of human life and nature.

There are examples in the histories of the kings which show this character. Sometimes a person whom the king favored the most was kept back from being the prime minister. This did not mean that it was not the wish of the king; it only meant that the king considered the sympathy and admiration he had for the person more than the prime-ministership. In other aspects one sees it. The king did not speak to a person for a long time; this did not mean that the king disfavored him; it only meant that the king knew that he would understand. There are instances when the patience of saints and sages has been tried to the uttermost. The pain and suffering that the spiritual souls have sometimes gone through, has been greater than the average person's. Behind this indifference there are many reasons.

Then one sees the other part of kingliness—that those who, sometimes, the king cared little for, were graciously received and amply rewarded. The ordinary mind could not conceive of the reason behind. The one who is responsible for his subjects, as a king, he understood rightly, like a gardener who knows which plant to rear and which tree had better be cut out of the garden. In spite of all opposition from all around, the kings have held to their idea, conscious of their duty. So it is with God.

But, king apart, even the manner and method of a responsible person is not always understood by another whose responsibility is not the same, so how can man always understand the ways of God—the only King in the true sense of the word, before Whom all other kings are nothing but imitations? It is the Kingship of God which manifests in the blossoming of every soul. When a soul arrives at its full bloom, it begins to show the color and spread the fragrance of the Divine Spirit of God.

The Birth of God

The reason why the soul seeks for the God-Ideal is that it is dissatisfied with all that momentarily satisfies it. All beauty, goodness and greatness which man attributes to God is something he admires and seeks through life. He admires these things in others, and strives to attain them for himself; and when, at the end of examination, he finds that all that he touches as good, great, or beautiful falls short of that perfection which is his soul's seeking, he then raises his eyes towards the sky and seeks for the One Who has beauty, goodness, and greatness, which is God. The one who does not seek for God, he has, in the end of his journey of illusion, a disappointment, for through the whole journey he did not find the perfection of beauty, goodness, and greatness on the earth, and he neither believed nor expected to meet such an ideal in heaven. All disappointments, which are the natural outcome of this life of illusion, disappear when once a person has touched the God-Ideal, for what one seeks after in life, one finds in God.

Now the question is: all beauty, goodness and greatness, however small and limited, can be found on the earth, but where can the same be found in the Perfection called God? This may be answered that what is first necessary is the belief that there is such a Being as God, in Whom goodness, beauty, and greatness are perfect.

In the beginning it will seem nothing but a belief; but in time, if the belief is kept in sincerity and faith, that belief will become like the egg of the phoenix, out of which the magic bird is born. It is the birth of God which is the birth of the soul. Every soul seeks for happiness, and after running after all objects which, for the moment, seem to give happiness, finds out that nowhere is there perfect happiness except in God. This happiness cannot come by merely believing in God. Believing is a process. By this process the God within is awakened and made living. It is the living of God which gives happiness. When one sees the injustice, the falsehood, the unfriendliness of human nature, and to what degree this nature develops, and that it culminates in tyranny of which individuals and the multitude become victims, there seems to be only one Source, and that is the center of the whole life, which is God, in Whom there is the place of safety from it all, and the source of peace, which is the longing of every soul.

Three Steps

The God-Ideal is meant to waken in the soul God, that it may realize His Kingship. It is this which is suggested in the prayer of Christ where it is said, "Thy Kingdom come, Thy Will be done." It is on this realization that the Kingdom of God comes; and what follows is that His Will is then done. But when a person does not know who is the king, he does not know what is the kingdom.

The kingdoms of the earth, from the time man has evolved so as to understand his affairs, have been established. Where man has learned the first lesson, when he first knew what a king means, what a kingdom means, he knew that there was someone whose command was obeyed by all, great and small, in the kingdom; who is the upraiser and the judge of all those who deserve honor and respect, who possess a treasure in the kingdom; who is as a mother and father of his subjects. Once this was learned, it gave the person an education to understand what a king means, as a child, after playing with her dolls, begins to understand the cares of the household.

The next step was taken in the spiritual path when the spiritual hierarchy was recognized. The Prophet or the high priest was recognized, representing the spiritual head. Then there was the hierarchy. In this way the next step was taken with the realization that it is not the outer environments, money and possession, which make a king, but it is the spiritual realization which can make a person greater than a king with all his kingly surroundings. This was proved to people when the king, who was accepted as the principal and head of the community, went before the high priest with bent head, and knelt down in the place of prayer. This gave the next lesson—that kingship is not in outer wealth, but in spirituality; that even the king stands humbly at the door of the God-realized man.

When once this step was taken, then there was the third step, which was to see that the high priest—considered as such even by the king—knelt down and bent his head low to the Lord, King of humanity, showing his greatness as dust before God, to Whom alone belongs all greatness. When the greatness of God was realized, God was glorified and the purpose of aristocracy was fulfilled, for it was nothing but a rehearsal before the battle. Once man realized that it is God alone before Whom man should bow, it is God alone Who really is rich and all are poor, it is God alone Whose wisdom and justice are perfect—then before him the kingship of the king and the holiness of the high priest faded away; before him remained only one King, the King of Kings; on Him he depended, and under Him he sought refuge under all the different circumstances in life.

After one had taken these three steps towards the goal, he found the goal to be quite different from the way that he had taken it, and the goal was the finding out the traces of that King within himself; a spark of that divine light which is the illumination of one's own heart; a ray of that Sun which is the light of the whole universe. And so self-realization developed, in which the soul found that wisdom, illumination, and peace which was the purpose of the God-Ideal.

God the Infinite

The Infinite God is the Self of God, and all that has manifested under name and form is the outward aspect of God. When we take all the forms existing and all the names put together, it becomes one form which is the Form of God. In other words, all names are the Name, and all forms are the Form of God. But as God is One, His Form is also One, and that is the sum total of all names and forms; there is no thing or being which is not the Being of God. In order to teach this, the wise have said there is God in everything, God is in every being. Many have wondered if He is in everything, how does He live in everything, and as what; if He is in man, where is He to be found, and what part of man's being is to be considered God? Many answers may be given, yet no answer will satisfy, for the true answer is, that all is God and God is all: none exists save He. And the question: "What are we then?" may be answered by the phrase in the Bible, that "we live and move and have our being in God." God is we, but we are not gods. The difference between God and our being is not of the Being; in Being, God and we are one. The difference is in our limitation and in the perfection of God.

How are we to conceive of the idea of God, the Absolute? We are not meant to conceive of that. We, as limited beings, are not able to know perfection, but perfection itself knows perfection. We can imagine and make a God of our own, to make God intelligible to us, to make it easy for us to advance on the spiritual path, and as we advance, the Unlimited Being, working through us, makes His own way and realizes His perfection, for in this realization He only realizes Himself, which is not at all difficult for Him.

Man thinks that religion or philosophy or mysticism, all this he has learned as he has evolved. Yes, it is true, but the result of all this learning and evolution is realized to a certain degree, not only by unevolved human beings, but even by the animals and birds. They all have their religion, and they all worship God in their own way. The birds, while singing in the forest, feel that exaltation even more than man feels it after he has worshiped. God, for all men who join in the prayers may not be so sincere as the birds in the forest; not one of them says its prayers without sincerity. If a soul were wakened to feel what they feel when singing in the forest at dawn, he would know that their prayer is even more exalting than his own, for their prayer is more natural. The godly, therefore, worship their God with Nature, and in this manner of worship they experience perfect exaltation as the result of their prayer. Man thinks he is able to meditate and that he can concentrate, but he cannot do better meditation and concentration than the animals and birds in the forest. The cobra attracts its food by a thought. There are certain cobras whose food comes and falls into their mouth. They fast patiently for a long time, not worrying about the food for the morrow. There are men who, on the contrary, are anxiously busy about their breakfast: they are not even certain of their luncheon. They have no confidence in their own power nor faith in the providence of God.

In short, spirituality is attained by all beings, not only by man but by the beasts and the birds, and each has its own religion, its principle, its law, and its morals. For instance, a bird, whose honor it is to fly over the heads of those who walk on the earth, feels it beneath its dignity to be touched by an earthly being: it feels it is polluted. And if this bird is touched once by a human being, its fellow creatures will not rest till they have killed it, for it is outcast for them; they dwell in the air and it is their dignity to be so. The study of Nature is not only of interest for the student of science; the one who treads the path of spirituality, for him the study of Nature is of immense interest. Man will find in the end of his search in the spiritual line that all beings, including trees and plants, rocks and mountains, are all prayerful, and all attain to that spiritual perfection which is the only longing of all souls.

God's Dealings with Us

Mankind has a tendency to consider all that is pleasant to be from the mercy of God, and all that is unpleasant, either from the wrath of God or not from God at all, thinking: "God is just and merciful." Really speaking, under all pleasant and unpleasant experiences in life, there is God's goodness and mercy and justice hidden. We call things unjust when we cannot see their justice; things are unpleasant to us when the standard of our pleasure is limited; things appear unmerciful to us when we restrict mercy in limitations. But sometimes things that do not seem to us just are just in their real nature; things unmerciful many times have mercy hidden behind them. Therefore, all that comes from God the Sufi takes with resignation, seeing and recognizing in it His mercy, goodness, and justice.

We, the children on earth, are as children in all our evolution through life before our Heavenly Father; and our action, in ignorance of this fact, is as the action of a little child. If the parents give him sweets, he takes it as their kindness; if they give him bitter medicine, he considers it wrath on their part, not knowing that in giving the bitter medicine their kindness is just the same. There are many things that we think are good for us; in fact, they may be the worst for our life. One's not being able to obtain a certain position which he wanted; one's not being able to settle in a town where he desired to; one's not being able to visit a city that he wished to see; one's not being able to attain the wealth he wished for—all such unpleasant experiences make one discontented; and if he has not enough faith, he begins to think that there is no such thing as God. If we would only think how perfect is the mechanism of the infant's body, and how it works in such order, we should see and realize that there is some Power behind, with full wisdom and understanding, that sets all things going harmoniously, and the whole mechanism of the universe also in the same way.

There is a story that Moses had sought the association of Khidr, the guiding angel of all seeking souls, and had requested him to be allowed to follow his path. Khidr said, "No, Moses. Teach the law that is given you; our way is complex." After great persistence on the part of Moses, Khidr complied with his request, on one condition: "You must not interfere with my works, by any means, in any way." When, on the seashore, they saw a little child drowning, caught by a wave, and the mother calling loudly for help, Moses wished to run to help them, and he wanted Khidr to do the same. Khidr said, "I have told you not to interfere with my works." Moses said, "Oh, would you allow an innocent child to be drowned like this when you can help? How unkind!" Khidr said, "Think of your promise, and do not say another word." They went farther, and took a boat to some port, and while in the boat Khidr began to enlarge the holes that were already in the boat. Moses said, "Oh, how unkind! Anyone who will sit in the boat will be drowned!" Khidr said, "It does not matter. Think of your promise, and do not say one word more." Upon Moses' great persistence in asking him to explain what it all meant, Khidr said, "The child that was drowning would have brought many families to destruction; therefore, it was meant by God that, before he became able to do so, he should be drowned. We have done nothing but allow the Will of God to take its course. And the boat in which I made the holes, when it will return, will carry thirty robbers who intend to destroy so many lives in a certain village, to accomplish their aim of robbery. It was meant by God that, as they have prepared themselves to destroy innocent lives, they may be destroyed before they can do so." This shows the meaning of a Sufi verse:

> *The Controller of the world knows how to control it,*
> *Whom He should rear and whom He should cut off.*

Dependence Upon God

Dependence is matter and independence is the spirit. The independent spirit becomes dependent through manifestation. When One becomes many, then each part of the One, being limited, strives to be helped by the other part, for each part finds itself imperfect. Therefore, we human beings, however rich with the treasures of heaven and earth, are poor in reality, because of our dependence upon others. The spiritual view makes one conscious of this fact, and the material view blinds man, who then shows independence and indifference to his fellow man. Pride, conceit, and vanity are the outcome of this ignorance. There are moments when even the king has to depend upon a most insignificant person. Often one needs the help of someone before whom one has always been proud and upon whom one has always looked with contempt. As individuals depend upon individuals, so the nations and races depend upon one another. As no individual can say, "I can get on without another person," so no nation can say, "We can be happy while another nation is unhappy." But an individual or a multitude depends most upon God, in Whom we all unite. Those who depend upon the things of the earth certainly depend upon things that are transitory, and they must someday or other lose them. Therefore, there remains only one object of dependence, that is, God, Who is not transitory, and Who always is and will be. Sa'adi has said, "He who depends upon Thee will never be disappointed."

No doubt it is the most difficult thing to depend upon God. For an average person, who has not known or seen, who never had any knowledge of such a personality existing as God, but has only heard in church that there exists Someone in the heavens, Who is called God, and has believed it, it is difficult to depend entirely upon Him. A person can hope that there is a God, that by depending upon Him he will have his desire fulfilled; a person can imagine that there can be Someone Whom people call God, but for him also it is difficult to depend entirely upon God. It is for them that the Prophet has said, "Tie your camel and trust in God." It was not said to Daniel, "Take a sword and go among the lions." One imagines God, another realizes God; there is a difference between these two persons. The one who imagines can hope, but he cannot be certain. The one who realizes God, he is face to face with his Lord, and it is he who depends upon God with certainty. It is a matter of struggling along on the surface of the water, or courageously diving deep, touching the bottom of the sea. There is no greater trial for a person than dependence upon God. What patience it needs, besides the amount of faith it requires, to be in the midst of this world of illusion and yet to be conscious of the existence of God! To do this, man must be able to turn all that is called life into death, and to realize in what is generally called death—in that death—the true life. This solves the problem of false and real.

Divine Grace

There is a saying that the one who troubles much about the cause is far removed from the cause. Many wonder: "If I am happy in life, what is the cause of it? If I am sorry in life, what is the cause of it? Is it my past life from where I have brought something which brings me happiness or unhappiness, or is it my action in this life which is the cause of my happiness or unhappiness?" And one can give a thousand answers and at the same time one cannot satisfy the questioner fully. When people think much about the law, they forget about love. When they think that the world is constructed according to a certain law, then they forget the Constructor Who is called in the Bible *Love*; God is Love.

In the first place, when we see from morning till evening man's selfish actions, whether good or bad actions, we see that he is not entitled to any happiness or anything good coming to him. And that shows that God does not always exact according to a certain law. He does not weigh your virtue on one side of the scale and His grace on the other, and exchange His grace for man's virtues. The Divine Being apart, man in his friendship, in his kindness, in his favor and disfavor, does he always exact what the other one is, or is doing? No. A friend admires his friend for his goodness and defends him for his wrongdoings. Does he not forget the law when there comes friendship? He forgets it. So man, instead of using justice and reason, overlooks all that is lacking and wrong. Something right comes forward to cover it all, to forget it all, to forgive it all. A mother whose son is accused of having done something wrong, she knows he has done wrong and she knows he is against the law. At the same time there is something else in her which wishes to lift up, to clear away. She would spend anything, lose anything, sacrifice anything in order that her son might not be punished. When we see that in everyday life, according to his evolution, man has a tendency to forget, to forgive, to look at things favorably, to cover all that is ugly; if this tendency is in man, from where does it come? It comes from the source which is Perfection. There is God. It is most amusing to see how people make God and His actions mechanical and how for themselves they claim free will. They say: "I choose to do this," or "I choose to do that," and "I have the free will to choose." This is man's claim. And at the same time he thinks that God and all His works and the universe are a mechanism. It is all running automatically. Man denies that God has a free will, and he himself claims it.

People look at it in two ways. They say: "All that man does is recorded, and in accordance to that it is adjusted. On the Judgment Day, either he has the reward of his good deeds or the punishment for his wrong deeds." Others who are more philosophical and intellectual say: "It is not God but it is the law, the automatic working which brings about a result in accordance to the cause, and therefore, what man has done in his past life, he experiences in this life." And there is a third point of view, that it need not be the hereafter and that it need not be the life ahead, in which man can have the experience and the result of his deeds, but that every day is his Judgment Day and that every day brings the result of his deeds. That is true also. There is no doubt that the world is constructed on a certain law, that the whole creation works according to a certain law. And yet it is not all. There is love beyond it, and it is the Prophets of all ages who have recognized that part of God's working and have given man that consolation and hope that in spite of our faults and shortcomings we will reach heaven. There is the Grace of God. Many know the Grace of God, and what does it mean? It means a wave of favor, a rising of love, a manifestation of compassion which sees no particular reason. One may say: "Does God close His eyes? Why must it be like this?" But in human nature we see the same thing. The divine nature can be recognized by human nature. Ask a lover who loves someone: "What is the beauty of that person? What is in that person that makes you love her?" He may try to explain: "It is because this person is kind, or because this person is beautiful, or because this person is good, or because this person is compassionate, or intellectual, or learned." But that is not the real cause. If really he knows what makes him love, he will say: "Because my beloved is beloved; that is the reason. There is no other reason." One can give a reason for everything. One can say: "I pay this person because he is good in his work; I pay for this stone because it is beautiful; but I cannot give a reason why I love; there is no reason for it." Love stands beyond law, beyond reason. The love of God works beyond reason, that Divine Love which is called the Grace of God; no piety, no spirituality, no devotion can attract it. No one can say: "I will draw the Divine Grace." God apart, can anyone say in this world: "I shall draw the friendship of someone." No one can say this. This is something which comes by itself. No one can command or attract it, or compel anyone to be his friend. It is natural. God's Grace is God's Friendship, God's Grace is God's Love, God's Compassion. No one has the power to draw it, to attract it; no meditation, no spirituality, no good action can attract it. There is no commercial business between God and man;

God stands free from rules which humanity recognizes. That aspect makes him the Lord of his own creation, as the wind blows, as the wind comes when it comes, so the Grace of God comes when it is its time to come.

I have heard people say, "I am ill," or "I am suffering," or "I am going through a difficulty," or "Things go wrong because of my Karma of the past." I say: "If it is so or if it is not so, your thinking about it makes it still worse; everything that one acknowledges to be, it becomes worse because one acknowledges it." That Karma which could be thrown away in one day's time, by acknowledging it, will keep with a person all his life. Some people think that they suffer or that they go through pain according to the law of Karma. But when the thought of the Grace of God comes and when one realizes the real meaning of the Grace of God, one begins to rise above it, and one begins to know that, "My little actions, my good deeds, all my good deeds I must collect in order to make them equal to God's mercy and compassion, His grace and His love, which He gives at every moment." God's compassion cannot be returned by all life's good actions. The relation of God and man apart, can one return a real thought of love, all a friend has done for us? We can love that friend, his loving kindness and his compassion. But we can never repay it. In all our life we cannot repay it.

Then we see the kindness and the compassion of God, which is always hidden from our view because we are always seeing what is lacking, the pain, the suffering, the difficulties. Man is so absorbed in them that he loses the vision of all the good that is there. We can never be grateful enough if we see like this, that it is not the law, but that it is the Grace of God which governs our life. And it is the trust and confidence in this Grace which not only consoles a person, but which lifts him and brings him nearer and nearer to the Grace of God.

Divine Grace is a loving impulse of God which manifests in every form, in the form of mercy, compassion, forgiveness, beneficence, and revelation. No action, however good, can command it; no meditation, however great, can attract it. It comes naturally, as a wave rising from the Heart of God, unrestricted or unlimited by any law. It is a natural impulse of God. When it comes, it comes without reason. Neither its coming nor its absence has any particular reason. It comes because it comes; it does not come because it does not come.

It is in Grace that God's Highest Majesty is manifested. While pouring out His Grace He stands on such a high pedestal, that neither law nor reason can touch it. Every blessing has a certain aspect, but Grace is a blessing which is not limited to a certain aspect, but manifests through all aspects. Grace is all-sided: health, providence, love coming from all those around you, inspiration, joy, peace.

The Will,
Human and Divine

The question of the will, human and divine, may be seen from two points of view, from the wisdom point of view and from the point of view of the ultimate Truth. If words can explain something, it is from the former point of view; the latter point of view allows no word to be spoken in the matter, for in the absolute Truth two do not exist, there is no such thing as two; there is One Alone. From the wisdom point of view, one sees one weaker, one stronger, and one has to give in to the power of the other. This one sees in all aspects of the creation. The little fish is eaten by the larger fish, but the little fish lives upon smaller fishes. So there is no one in this world so strong that he has not another stronger still, and there is no one in this world so weak that he has not another who is weaker still. The other thing one can think about, is the opposing conditions and situations which stand before a willing mind and a striving person like a stone wall, so that, with every wish to do something and to accomplish, one does not find his way. It is this experience which has made man say, "Man proposes, God disposes." The Hindu philosophers have called these two great powers, one of which is an intention and the other the power of destruction, by the names *Brahma*, the Creator, and *Shiva*, the Destroyer. The most wonderful part in this creation and destruction is that what Brahma creates in a thousand years, Shiva destroys in one moment. Since God is almighty, the wise see the Hand of God in the greater power, manifesting either through an individual or by a certain condition or situation, and instead of struggling too much against the difficulties in life, and instead of moaning over the losses which cannot be helped, they are resigned to the Will of God.

In short, every plan that a person makes, and his desire to accomplish that plan, is often an outcome of his personal will; and when his will is helped by every other will that he comes in contact with in the path of the attainment of a certain object, then he is helped by God. As every will goes in the direction of his will and so his will becomes strengthened, often a person accomplishes something which perhaps a thousand people could not have been able to accomplish. Then there is another person who has a thought, a desire, and finds opposition from every side; everything seems to go wrong, and yet he has the inner urge which prompts him to go on in the path of attainment. There also is the Hand of God behind his back, pushing him on, forward in his path, even though there might seem oppositions in the beginning of his strife—but all's well that ends well.

The saintly souls, who consider it as their religion to seek the pleasure of God and to be resigned to His will, are really blessed, for their manner is pleasing to everyone, for they are conscientious lest they may hurt the feeling of anyone, and if by some mistake they happen to hurt someone's feelings, they feel they have hurt God Whose pleasure they must constantly seek, for the happiness of their life is only in seeking the pleasure of God. They watch every person and every situation and condition, and their heart becomes so trained by constantly observing life keenly, as a lover of music whose ears become trained in time, who distinguishes between the correct and the false note. So they begin to see every desire that springs in their heart, if it is in accordance with the Will of God. Sometimes they know the moment the desire was sprung; sometimes they know when they have gone halfway in the path of its pursuit; and sometimes they know at the end of strife. But even then, at the end of it, their willingness to resign to the Will of God becomes their consolation, even in the face of disappointment. The secret of seeking the Will of God is in cultivating the faculty of sensing harmony, for harmony is beauty, and beauty is harmony. The lover of beauty in his further progress becomes the seeker of harmony, and by trying always to maintain harmony man will tune his heart to the Will of God.

Making God Intelligible

Sometimes the question is asked, "How can we make God intelligible?"

You can make a chair intelligible by touching, by looking at it, and seeing how it is made. You make a house intelligible by seeing how it is made. You can make a tree intelligible by seeing how it is: its stem, fruits, leaves, appearance, then what comes out of it. The word *intelligible* means through our senses we feel a thing, we know a thing, we have a conception of a thing; that is to make it intelligible. To make anything intelligible is to make a concrete conception of it.

And now the question is how to make God intelligible? It is impossible to make God intelligible, really. But, at the same time, it is in order to make God intelligible that the Egyptians made the Sphinx; it is in order to make God intelligible that the fire-worshipers offered homage to the sun; it is in order to make God intelligible that people have made idol worship, and it is also in order to make God intelligible that people esteemed their divine ideal with their devotion, as those worshipers of Jesus Christ. All these forms are attempts on the part of man to make God intelligible. Man can only make God intelligible in the form that seems to him the best. That form must be seen by him, must be imagined by him, and must be known by him. If he knows that form as a person, he calls it Christ, or some other name he gives to it. He makes him the king, because he thinks that the king is the greatest person. He gives him the throne and crown. He calls him the Master of the Day of Judgment, because he knows there is no justice in this world, so he thinks God must be the Judge. He thinks all that is beautiful, surrounds him with angels, conceives the form of angels as human beings. He pictures God in the form of man. There have been attempts of putting all sorts of things on one being. The Chinese used to make a dragon to which all things were attached— fish, lion, tiger, man, everything that existed—in order to make one form intelligible to serve as a symbol suggesting and teaching many things. Every effort is a failure, but every effort to make God intelligible is worthwhile.

Now there have been two stages of making God intelligible. One stage was idol worship, and the other stage was ideal worship. One was the primitive stage, a stage in which God was made manifest in an unusual form, but at the same time intelligible. A further stage was that they made God an ideal. Instead of making Him a God of forms, they made Him a God of attributes. And then they said all the beauty, goodness, wisdom, and justice belong to Him. All things that we can conceive in our mind, we give those things to God, and consider all those things in God in their perfection. That is the highest form of making God intelligible. That all that our intelligence, our mind, thinks as beautiful, as good, as valuable, to see all that in perfection in One Being, and to idealize that Being as the greatest and the highest of all beings: that is what we call making God intelligible. But, at the same time, in the spiritual path that is the first step. In the religious path that is the last step; in the spiritual path that is the first step.

Man's Relation to God

Man's relation to God may be likened to the relation of the bubble and the sea. Man is of God, man is from God, man is in God, as the bubble is from water, of water, and in water. So much the same and yet so different! The bubble is different and the sea is different and there is no comparison between them. So, though God and man are not different, yet there is such a difference that there is no comparison. Hafiz says, "What comparison between earth and heaven?" The same reason makes man small before God, as the bubble is small before an ocean, and yet it is not apart from the ocean, nor is it of any other element than the ocean. Therefore Divinity is in man as in God. The Divinity of Christ means the Divinity of man, although Divinity itself is the ideal.

The word *divine* has its origin in Sanskrit. It is from *Deva*, which means the same—divine. And yet the root of this word means light. That means that the divine is that part of being which is illuminated by the light within. Therefore, though in man, the light is hidden, not disclosed. He is not divine. If the hidden light were divine, then the stone could be divine too, for the spark of fire is hidden in the rock. All life is one, no doubt, and all names and forms are of the same life. But that part of life out of which springs light, illuminating itself and its surroundings and bringing to its notice its own being, is divine; for in this is the fulfillment of the purpose of the whole creation, and every activity is directed to bringing about the same purpose. How calmly the mountains and hills seem to be waiting for some day to come. If we went near them and listened to their voice, they would tell us this. And how eagerly the plants and the trees in the forest seem to be waiting for some day, for some hour to come, the hour of the fulfillment of their desire! If we could only hear the words they say! In animals, in birds, in the lower creation, the desire is still more intense and still more pronounced. The seer can see it when his glance meets their glance. But the fulfillment of this desire is in man: the desire that has worked through all aspects of life and brought forth different fruits, yet preparing a way to reach the same Light which is called divinity. But even man, whose right it is, cannot touch it unless he acquire the knowledge of the Self, which is the essence of all religions.

It is easy to claim that, "I am God!"; but what is it? Is it not insolence on the part of man, who is subject to illness, death, and disease? It is bringing the highest ideal of God on the lowest plane. It is like the illusion of the bubble saying, "I am the sea! I am the sea!" when his own conscience, as well as everybody else's, sees that he is a bubble. And again it is blind on the part of man, however righteous and pious he may be, to say, "I am separate, God is separate. I am on earth, God is in heaven." He will pray and worship a thousand years and not reach near God. Since, according to the idea of an astronomer, it would take so many hundreds of years to reach a certain planet, how could one reach so high as the Abode of God, which is supposed to be still higher and farther than anything else? No man has a right to claim divinity as long as he is conscious of his limited self. He only, who is so absorbed in the contemplation of the Perfect Being that his limited self is lost from his sight, could say this, which in many cases is not said. It is at this time that man closes his lips, lest he might say a word that might offend the ears of the people in the world. "O bird, cry gently, for the ears of the beloved are tender!" And if anyone, such as Mansur, has claimed divinity, it is in that wine of divine Life that intoxicated him, and the secret came out of him as it comes from a drunken man, which, if he had been sober, he would not have given out.

The wise realize the Divine Being in the loss of the thought of self, and melt in Him, and become absorbed in Him, and enjoy the peace that they can derive from the Divine Life, but live in the world gently, meekly and thoughtfully, just like every man. It is the unwise who show themselves too wise. And with the increase of wisdom that beauty of innocence comes that makes the wise the friend of everyone, both stupid and wise. It is the stupid who cannot agree with the wise, but the wise can agree with the stupid as well as with the wise. He can become both, while the stupid man is what he is.

Divine Manner

In the terms of the Sufis the divine manner is called *Akhlak-i Allah*. Man thinks, speaks, and acts according to the pitch to which his soul is tuned. The highest note he could be tuned to is the divine note, and it is that pitch, once man arrives at it, that he begins to express the manner of God in everything he does. And what is the manner of God? It is the kingly manner, a manner which is not even known to the kings, for it is a manner which only the King of the heaven and of the earth knows. And that manner is expressed by the soul who is tuned to God, a manner which is void of narrowness, a manner which is free from pride and conceit, the manner which is not only beautiful but beauty itself, for God is beautiful and He loves beauty. The soul who is tuned to God, also becomes as beautiful as God, and begins to express God through all that it does, expressing in life the divine manner. Why is it a kingly manner? By the word *kingly* we only signify someone who possesses power and wealth in abundance. The soul tuned to God, before whom all things fade away and in whose eyes the importance of all little things, of which every person thinks so much, is lessened, that soul begins to express the divine manner in the form of contentment. It might seem to an ordinary person that to this soul nothing matters, no gain is exciting, no loss is alarming; if anyone praises, it has no consequence: if anyone blames, it does not matter to him; the honor and the insult, this all to him is a game, for in the end of the game, neither the gain is a gain nor the loss is a loss; it was only a pastime.

One might think, What does such a person do to the others; what good is he to those around him? That person, for the others and those around him, is a healing; that person is an influence for uplifting souls—the souls who are suffering from the narrowness and from the limitation of human nature. For human nature is not only narrow and limited, but it is foolish and it is tyrannous. The reason is that the nature of life is intoxicating. Its intoxication makes people drunken. And what does the drunken man want? He wants his drink: he does not think about another. In this life there are so many liquors that man drinks: the love of wealth, passion, anger, possession; man is not only satisfied with possessing earthly properties, but he also wishes to possess those whom he pretends to love, and in this way proves to be tyrannous and foolish. For all things of this world that man possesses, he does not in reality possess them, only he is possessed by them, be it wealth or property or a friend or position or rank. The soul with divine manner is therefore sober compared with the drunken man of the world: it is this soberness that produces in him that purity which is called Sufism, and it is through that purity that God reflects in his mirror-like soul. For the soul who reflects God, nothing frightens; he is above all fright, for he possesses nothing, and all fright is connected with the possessions that man has. Does it mean that he leaves the world and goes and passes his life in the caves of the mountain? Not in the least. He may have the wealth of the whole world in his possession, he may have the kingdom of the whole universe under him, but nothing binds him, nothing ties him, nothing frightens him, for that only belongs to him which is his own. And when his soul is his own, all is his own, and what belongs to him cannot be taken away. And if anyone took it away, it is he himself who did it. He is his friend and his foe, and so there is no longer a pain or suffering, a complaint or grudge; he is at peace, for he is at home, be he on earth or be he in heaven.

The difference between God and man is that God is omniscient and man only knows of his own affairs. As God is omniscient, He loves all and His interest is in all; and so it is with the godly soul. The divine personality, expressed through the godly soul, shows itself in its interest for all, whether known or unknown to that soul. His interest is not only for another, because of his kind nature or of his sympathetic spirit; he does not take interest in another person, in his welfare and well-being because it is his duty, but because he sees in another person *himself*. Therefore, the life and interest of another person to the godly soul is as his own. In the pain of another person the godly soul sorrows; in the happiness of another person the godly soul rejoices. So the godly soul, who has almost forgotten himself, forgets also the remaining part of the self in taking interest in others. From one point of view it is natural for the godly soul to take interest in another. The one who has emptied himself of what is called self in the ordinary sense of the word is only capable of knowing the condition of another. He sometimes knows, perhaps, more than the person himself, as a physician knows the case of his patient.

Divine manner, therefore, is not like that of the parents to their children, of a friend toward his beloved friend, of a king to his servant, or of a servant to his master. Divine manner consists of all manners; it is expressive of every form of love; and if it has any peculiarity, that peculiarity is one, and that is divine. For in every form of love and affection, there somewhere the self is hidden, which asks for appreciation, for reciprocity, for recognition. The divine manner is above all this. It gives all and asks nothing in return in any manner or form, in this way proving the Action of God through man.

The Spiritual Hierarchy

The Spiritual Hierarchy

The idea of the spiritual hierarchy has been a question which has always been discussed in all ages, and especially at this time, when people have their conceptions much more separate and different, along spiritual lines, than before. The spiritual hierarchy is not man's imagination; it is not only a poetic idea, but it is as real as one's own being. Among hills and mountains there are small mountains and there are big mountains; among rivers there are larger and smaller rivers; and in all things of Nature one finds the evidence of Nature's hierarchy. What gives us the best picture of life is the heavens, with the planets, and the sun apart as a light- and life-giver. When we consider all the planets, including the moon, we shall find they are all receptacles of light, and they all reflect the light of the sun according to their capacity. The moon functions as a receptacle of the same light to the greatest degree. According to the mystical point of view, if it were not for the moon the whole cosmos would go to pieces, for the reason that the central currents of the sun are functioning in the moon, which reflects the light of the sun in fullness. Only the difference is that, as it is the reflection of the sun—although in its fullness—it has finer currents of light, it is soft and cooling, attractive, and its light is beautiful. Therefore the light of the sun is called *jelal* by the Sufis, and the light of the moon *jemal*. The former expresses power, and the latter beauty. The former is creative; the latter is responsive. Suppose, then, if the sun has the light, then the moon possesses the light of the sun, not its own. If God is the Knower and the All-wise, the one who gives His Message gives God's knowledge, not his own; it is the light of the sun; so it is with the Messengers at all times. People have heard them speak, and therefore they call it the Message of Buddha, or of Christ, or of Muhammad; but, really speaking, the Message was of God.

All souls in the world are the receptacles of God's Message—not only human beings, but even the lower creation. All objects and all conditions convey to us the Message of the One and Only Being. But the difference is that, although they convey the Message of God, they do not know it; they are not conscious of it. Not only objects are unconscious, but even human beings are unconscious. If they only knew that there is nothing in this world which is not the instrument of God! As there are more useful and less useful objects, so there are more and less important human beings. If they were all equal, there would not have been the diversity of different ranks and positions in a state; there would not have been generals or colonels in the army—all soldiers; there would not have been high and low notes on the piano, but all one key, one note, one sound; there would not have been different rooms in the house—every room would have been a drawing-room. But it shows that it is the necessity of life that there should be a hierarchy—hierarchy by election or hierarchy by appointment—for the world cannot exist without it. Aristocracy and democracy are not two things, but one. There is but one chief thing, which is hierarchy. When it is right, it is called aristocracy; when it goes wrong, and when there comes a new spirit to rebuild it, this process is a state of democracy. It is natural that man is agitated with one thing when he wants to build another thing. He revolts against everything that was before, and so, in rebuilding, this revolting spirit often acts to his disadvantage.

As externally there is a system of government, so inwardly there is a system of government. One can see this government in every family also. There is a king in every family; there are ministers, counselors, partakers of his responsibility, and servants who are paid for their work. Taking the whole universe as one whole, there is also a system of government, as there is a system of government in the sky; there is the sun; then there is the moon, which is directly focused to the sun; and there are the principal planets, which surround it; and there are the stars. And on the model of the heaven the inner and outer governments of the earth are arranged. In the same way man's body is arranged: there is one principal factor; then there are working factors, as servants; then principal ministers; and when one takes the existence of man, from his soul to his body, it is one complete kingdom, which constitutes all the necessary officials and servants, making one's being as a kingdom. In that way it shows that the king will always exist. No democratic view, however much against the aristocratic form, will ever succeed in life without forming the kingdom. The difference is that, if he will not call the one *king*, he will name him *president*.

In the spiritual hierarchy, there are seven grades of spiritual souls who form the spiritual standard; and each grade is divided into two classes, *jelal* and *jemal*. And, descending from the combination of these two spirits, there comes a third line as a central line, which is the spirit of prophecy and which is called the Spirit of Guidance. It has never been necessary for any of these members of the hierarchy to acclaim themselves, especially for the reason that in this world of falsehood there are false claims; and even the real claims, in the worldly life, are no more true than false; and also as there has been no reason why the claims should be made, since the holders of these offices can serve the purpose better by being silent than by announcing themselves as So-and-so. And, when every office in the world brings to man a certain amount of vanity, and as vanity is the greatest enemy of spiritual people; and as there is the jealousy of human nature always at work, and as competition and rivalry are the very source that give stimulus to the life in the world, the office has always been concealed by the spiritual officeholders, except by the teachers who had to give the Message of God to people and teach them. And how many in the world would not believe unless they knew he was the office bearer from God!

The teachers had their lives as the example of their office; except that, they had no other evidence. Miracles are known afterwards; legends are formed afterwards; poems are made afterwards; temples are built afterwards; following has increased afterwards; their words have been valued afterwards. But during their lifetime they met with nothing but opposition and the constant change of the followers, agreeing one day, disagreeing another day; and all sorts of difficulties they have suffered, even such as crucifixion. The teacher's position is more delicate than that of the Master, because he must claim, and be among people. And being among people is to be as a bird of a different forest having arrived in a strange land, and all other birds, finding him different from them, wish to fight him and torture him, and wish to kill him. That has been the condition of the Prophet in all times, and the same will always be. The last One left a warning for the coming One, which was this: that prophecy was sealed. He did not mean by this that the work of the Spirit of Guidance was sealed. It was a clue to the Successor, now that the claim was sealed, that the work must be done without a claim, and it is the work that is done that should prove its genuineness, instead of a claim.

According to the Sufi conception, there are several degrees distinguished as different stages of responsiveness; in other words, of higher initiation. Among them there are five principal ones: *Wali, Ghous, Qutub, Nabi, Rasul,* the sign of *Rasul* being the crescent, which represents a responsive heart. People call them Masters, but they are in reality pupils; for, in point of fact, no one in the world is a Master save God. Man's privilege is to become a greater pupil. Therefore none of the Great Ones have called themselves Masters, nor have they considered themselves to be so. What they have known in their lives is the privilege of opening their hearts wider and wider to reflect the light of the Master, Who is God Himself. The progress of these high Initiates is in their responsiveness, for they have never connected themselves with what they have expressed.

Very often parents say something to their child in which there is the Voice of God; very often a kind friend suggests something to his friend, out of his love and sympathy, which happens to be a Message of God; sometimes a teacher says an inspiring word, which is as a word coming direct from God; even from an innocent child a word comes which comes as a warning from God; for all faces, are His faces, and from all lips it is His Word that comes, whenever it comes. But those who can respond to Him, they become as His appointed servants. People call them Chosen Ones; God has chosen all, for all souls are near to the Creator. But the soul who is attached to the lips of God as a horn becomes the herald of His Message, and through his lips what comes is not his words, but the Message of God.

Seven Grades of the Spiritual Hierarchy

There are seven grades recognized by the Sufis of those in the spiritual hierarchy: *Pir, Buzurg, Wali, Ghous, Qutub, Nabi, Rasul.* These are the degrees which come from the inner initiations—the inner initiations to which one becomes entitled on having the outer initiations which are necessary. It is beyond words to express what inner initiation means and in what form it is given. Those to whom the inner initiation is unknown may explain it as a dream or as a vision, but in reality it is something higher and greater than that. I can only explain it by saying that the definite changes which take place during one's journey through the spiritual path are initiations, and it is these initiations which include man in the spiritual hierarchy.

In the life of a Saint or a Master there are five degrees known, and in the two last degrees the progress of the Saint and of the Master is silent, but in the life of a Prophet these seven degrees manifest to view. For a Saint or a Master there is one facility—that he can do his work by avoiding the notice of the world. But the life of the Prophet necessitates his coming into the world, and thus, as he progresses from grade to grade through his life, he cannot very well cover himself, however much he may want to, from the gaze of the world, though the Sage of every category—Saint, Master, or Prophet—and every degree, always prefers not being known to the world; and as he progresses, so that desire increases more. But it is not only out of modesty or humbleness, but also for the protection of the spiritual ideal which is developed in him, for it attracts dangers of all sorts by being exposed to the common gaze. All beauty is veiled by nature, and the higher the beauty, the more it is covered. And that makes it easy for a wise person to find out the difference between a true Prophet and a false Prophet, for one beats his drums and the other tries to keep in the background—if only his work in the world would let him keep back. It is his efforts in accomplishing something that bring him to the notice of the world. However, his longing is to be unknown, for the One who really deserves being known is God alone.

The work of the *Pir* is helping individuals toward the unfoldment of their soul. The work of the *Buzurg* is to help by the power of his soul those who wish to advance spiritually.

Wali is the Initiate whose will has come close to the Divine Will, and he shows it in the harmony which reigns in his own life—harmony with friends, and he himself will be in harmony with the adversary also. He shows harmony with the changing weather and its different influences, and is in harmony with all he eats and drinks. He is in harmony with the place he lives and moves about in, and he harmonizes with all atmospheres. And so his will becomes the Will of God; in other words, the Will of God becomes his will. He controls a community, keeping it on the right track. He does that work, for which he is appointed, mostly in an unknown way. The greater a person is in spiritual advancement, the less assuming he becomes; and he avoids every show of piety or spirituality.

Ghous is the next grade of the Initiates. The influence of the *Ghous* is wider. He gives up his personality wholly to the Divine Guidance. Therefore in the district, wherever this *Ghous* may be, an atmosphere will be created of protection from all kinds of dangers caused by floods and storms and by plagues and famines; and he helps the spiritual well-being of a community.

Qutub is the third degree of a Master, of a still higher grade, whose mind becomes focused to the Divine Mind, and who has, to a smaller or greater extent, power over all elements and influence upon life. There is under him a dominion, in which he is responsible for the order and peace of souls. He governs spiritually a country or a nation.

Nabi is the apostle whose spirit reflects the Spirit of Guidance, called in Sanskrit *Bodhisattva*, whose work mainly is the giving of the Message in the form of warning, awakening, preaching, teaching, and inspiring those to whom he may be sent. He comes into the lives of those who are meant to be guided along the spiritual path. He is sent to the nations when the nations are meant to change their conditions. He is sent to a community or race to give warnings. He is meant to be a reformer in the times when a reformer is needed. He elevates individuals and bears a Divine Message.

Rasul is the World Messenger, who comes to the world for all the people in the time of the world's need, and brings with him that inspiration, influence, and power which will harmonize humanity. He may be a king or a pauper; in all conditions he will fulfill the purpose of his coming on earth. Answering the cry of humanity, he fulfills the purpose of his mission on earth.

The question: "Where does one receive the initiation of the higher orders?" may be answered that no man in the world has the power to give the above-said higher initiations. They are initiated by God Himself, and they prove their initiations, not in their claims, but in their works. The soul that rises to that stage where manhood finishes and Godhead begins, enters the initiation of the spiritual hierarchy. But the soul, which has risen to that stage, is neither man nor God. He is not God, because he is limited man; and he is not man, because he is God-conscious.

The Ways of the Wise

It is not easy to learn, and after learning, to practice, how to make life in the world with harmony and peace. The desire of every person in the world is to possess all he wants, whether it belongs to him or whether it belongs to anybody else. He wants all things to last, if they are any use to him; he wants all those dear and near to him should abide close to him; all he doesn't wish to see must be exiled from the town, and at the same time even the whole of nature must work to suit him: the cold must not be more than he wants, the heat must not exceed his desire, the rain must obey him, pain must not approach near. There must not be anything difficult in life and all things and people must be perfect in the perfection of God; everybody must act in life as he wishes them to; he alone must be the engineer and all others his machines. They must have all the endurance he demands of them; at the same time all must be as sensitive as he wants them to be. No one should move against his desire; not even a bird must fly in the sky, nor even a leaf must make a flutter: all under his command. He alone must live and all others must live, but under him. This attitude I have not spoken of someone in the world, but every individual. The world is a place where every individual wishes to be the king, so many kings and only one kingdom, and the whole tragedy of life is accounted for by this.

The wise, out of wisdom, make life easy. But among the wise there are two categories: one is the Master, the other is the Saint. The attitude of both in life is quite contrary. The attitude of the Saint is to feel sympathy for others and to see the difficulties of the situation in life of others as of himself, and to sacrifice his wants for the need of others, realizing that he knows that life is difficult, and those who are void of wisdom have still more difficulties as they know not how to surmount the difficulties of life. Out of his love, mercy and compassion he thus sacrifices his life to the service of his fellow man by making life easy for them.

In the first place he sees the worst enemy of his fellow man in himself, knowing that the nature of every ego is hostile, and by being resigned to the will of his fellow man, by sacrificing his life's advantages for his brother, he feels he has given his fellow man some relief that he could give him on his part. By practicing this moral through life at every step that a wise man takes, he becomes a source of happiness to all he meets and with whom he comes in contact in life, and his spirit becomes deepened in saintliness.

Then there is the way of the Master which is quite opposite. He conquers himself, he battles with life, he is at war with destiny, he crusades against all that seems wrong to him, he finds the key to the secrets unknown to him. Instead of being resigned to all conditions, all things, all people, he turns them to the shape that he wishes and molds as he likes the personalities which come in touch with him.

And yet neither of them, Saint or Master, comes to claim before the world, "Look at me—I am a Saint," "I am a Master," "I can do this," or "I am such a virtuous person," or "a good person." They keep themselves in humble guise, one like everybody in the world. It is not a claim, it is an action which proves the Master. And yet what do they care if the world acclaims them as a Saint or as a

Master? What benefit is it to them? It is only a benefit to the one who is false, because he is glad to be something he is not; he who is all does not wish that everybody should recognize him as such. A person with his riches knows that he is rich, he need not put on fifty rings to tell everybody how rich he is; but the one who puts on fifty rings is seldom rich. There is a beautiful simile known in India, that it is the empty vessel that makes the noise; when it is filled with water it makes no noise. In short, sincerity is the principal thing to attain in life. What little is gained sincerely and held unassumingly is worth much more than a greater gain void of sincerity, for it is a hill of sand; once the storm will come and blow it away. Verily, truth is the treasure that every soul is seeking.

The Master, the Saint,
the Prophet

There are three roads to spiritual attainment, which meet in the end at one junction. One road is of the Master; another comes from quite a different point, and is the road of the Saint; and the middle path between the two is of the Prophet. The path of the Master is a path of war—war with outer influences which prevent one from making one's way through life. The path of the Master wants self-discipline and will power to make headway through life. It is a path of accomplishment. All that the Master takes up, he accomplishes; all that the Master desires, he attains sooner or later. Yet the Master's one desire is spiritual attainment at its fullest. Therefore all other attainments, spiritual or material, are nothing before him other than many steps on a staircase. The struggle in the path of the Master is great; he has struggle all along. Every condition that meets him on the way to accomplishment is harder to get through than the condition before. No doubt, as he proceeds on the path of attainment, he gains power through struggle. The greater the struggle through life, the greater his power. He tunes personalities to the tone which would suit his orchestration. He has command over objects; he produces effects in objects, which are not there naturally. He can even rise to a state where he can command Nature, and the spiritual hierarchy is made of the Masters. For the world is ruled; it is governed. Although outward governments are different, inward government is the spiritual hierarchy. In the East such are called *Wali*, whose thought, whose feeling, whose glance, whose impulse, can move the universe. And the Master may advance gradually through the five principal stages of attainment, and may even arrive at the stage of *Rasul* in the end.

The path of the Saint is one of love, harmony, and beauty; ready to give, ready to sacrifice, ready to renounce, ready to give in and to yield. The saintly soul takes all insults as one would take something as a purifying process. He is resigned to every loss, for there is no loss without some gain and there is no gain which is without any loss; there is always a hidden loss in the gain and a gain in the loss. Renunciation is not difficult for that soul, for in renunciation that soul finds its freedom. No sacrifice is too great for the saintly soul, for it gives him happiness. Generosity that soul need not learn: it is its nature, its character. Modesty, humility, tolerance, forgiveness, are part of his being; he cannot do otherwise, for he knows no differently. Through this path, no doubt in the beginning the saintly soul finds difficulty. The path of the Saint has a constant battle with the self, for there is no end to the world's demands; in this world no one can be too good or too kind. The better one is, the more good is asked of one; the kinder one is, the more kindness is expected from one; and so it goes on through life. The happiness a saintly soul finds, through all the continual sacrifices that he makes as he goes through life, is in his will gradually becoming harmonized to the Will of God, so that God's Will and his will in time become one. And that happiness no one can imagine except the souls who have experienced the feeling of resignation through all the crosses that one has to meet in life. The spirit of a Saint results in being ined to the whole universe. He is in tune with the climates, with the weather, with nature, with animals and birds; he becomes in tune with the trees and plants, in tune with all atmospheres, with all human beings of various natures, because he becomes the keynote to the whole universe. All harmonize with him; the virtuous souls, the wicked souls, angels and devils; all become in tune. He becomes in harmony with every object, with every element; with those who have passed from this earth he is in tune; with those in the atmosphere he is in tune, and in tune with those who live on earth. The moral of a Saint is very difficult, but the spirit of the Saint is a benediction to himself and blessing to others.

The work of the Master is to protect individuals and protect the world. The work of the Master is to keep away all disasters that might come about, caused by the inharmony of the nature of individuals and of the collectivity. The work of the Master is to help the feeble but right, the weak but just, when he is in a situation where he is opposed by a powerful enemy. The work of the Saint is to console the wretched, to take under the wings of mercy and compassion those left alone in life, to bless the souls that come in his way.

The way of the Prophet is a more balanced way, for in the life of the Prophet there is a balance of these two attributes—the power of attainment and the patience to resign to the Will of God. So the Prophet is a warrior and a peacemaker, both at the same time. This line is called *kemal*, the perfect, or balanced. The work of the Prophet is not only his own spiritual attainment, but he has some certain service of great importance to perform. As the Prophet goes through the above said five stages, he acts on his way towards the fulfillment of his life's mission as a warner, as a healer, as a reformer, as a lawyer, as a teacher, as a priest, as a preacher. Therefore such service keeps the Prophet away from what his soul always craves for, and that is the solitude in the wilderness. He longs for one place, and he is put in another place. The soul who yearns constantly to fly away from the crowd is put, owing to his mission, in the very midst of the crowd. In this way the work of the Prophet in the world becomes as hard as if a person were asked to jump into the water and then come out dry. He must live in the world and not be of the world. However, it is the prophetic soul whose life's mission very often is to serve humanity in the time of its need, and it is the fulfillment of this service which makes him *Rasul*, the Messenger.

The Prophet is the Message bearer; the Prophet is master and a servant at the same time; the Prophet is a teacher and at the same time a pupil, for there is a great deal that he must learn from his experience through life, not in order to make himself capable to receive the Message, but in order to make himself efficient enough to give the Message. For God speaks to the Prophet in His divine tongue, and the Prophet interprets it in his turn in the language of men, making it intelligible to them, trying to put the finest ideas in the gross terms of worldly language. Therefore all that the Prophet comes to give to the world is not given in words, but all that cannot be given in words is given without words. It is given through the atmosphere; it is given by the presence; it is given by the great love that gushes forth from his heart; it is given in his kind glance; and it is given in his benediction. And yet the most is given in silence that no earthly sense can perceive. The difference between human language and divine words is this: that a human word is a pebble; it exists, but there is nothing further; the divine word is a living word, just like a grain of corn. One grain of corn is not one grain; in reality it is hundreds and thousands. In the grain there is an essence which is always multiplying, and which will show perfection in itself.

The Prophet

The Prophet is the manifestation of the same Spirit who can rightfully be called Alpha and Omega in its fullest expression, although the spirit of Alpha and Omega is in all beings—in a loving mother, in a kind father, in an innocent child, in a helpful friend, in an inspiring teacher. The Prophet is a mystic, and greater than a mystic; the Prophet is a philosopher, and greater than a philosopher; the Prophet is a poet, and greater than a poet; the Prophet is a teacher, and greater than a teacher; the Prophet is a seer, and greater than a Seer. Why greater? Because he has a duty to perform; together with the blessing that he brings upon earth.

In the terms of the Eastern people, the Prophet is termed *Paghambar*. There are also two other names, *Nabi* and *Rasul*; and although each of these names is expressive of the Prophet, yet each name is significant of a certain attribute of the Prophet: also each of those words denotes a certain degree of his evolution. *Paghambar* verbally means "the Message bearer," and this word is used for the Holy Ones who from time to time brought a Divine Message to a certain community, nation, or race, whenever there was need of wakening a certain people. The *Paghambar* has worked as an alarm to warn people of the coming dangers; the *Paghambar* has brought reforms to improve the condition of his people.

There are two steps in the life of the Messenger, one minor and the other major. One stage is when he begins to give the Message; the next stage is when the Message is fulfilled. *Nabi*, therefore, is the one who begins to give the Message; *Rasul* is the one who fulfills the Message.

Nabi is the Prophet who is not only for a certain section of humanity. Although he may live and move only in a limited region of the world, yet what he brings has its bearing upon the whole of humanity. It may not be fulfilled in his lifetime, but a day of fulfillment comes some time, even if it be in some centuries, that all he brought reaches the whole of humanity. *Rasul* is a term which denotes an advanced degree, where the Prophet has not only brought a Message to the world, but fulfilled his task during his lifetime, through all tests and trials that a Prophet is meant to meet in life.

The Prophet is an interpreter of the divine law in human tongue. He is an ambassador of the spiritual hierarchy, for he represents to humanity the illuminated souls who are known and unknown to the world, who are hidden and manifest, who are in the world or on the other side of the world. The Prophet is an Initiate and initiator, for he is an answer to the cry of humanity, of individuals, and of the collectivity; the one who sympathizes with those in pain, guides those in darkness, harmonizes those who are in conflict and brings peace to the world, which always, when excited with its activity of centuries, loses its equilibrium.

The Prophet can never tell the ultimate Truth, which only his soul knows and no words can explain. His mission is, therefore, to design and paint and make the picture of the Truth in words that may be intelligible to mankind. The bare Truth not every man can see. If he can see, he needs no more teaching. The Prophet, so to speak, listens to the words of God in the language of God, and he interprets the same words in the human tongue. He speaks to every man in his own language; he converses with every man, standing on his own plane. Therefore he has little chance to disagree, unless there were someone who wanted disagreement and nothing else; there he cannot help.

Besides the words which even an intellectual person can speak, the Prophet brings the love and the light which is the food of every soul. The very presence of the Prophet may make a person see things differently, and yet he may not know that it was because of the Prophet. He may only think that that which was not clear to him, or for a moment seemed difficult to him, is now right and clear. For the Prophet is a living light, a light which is greater in power than the sun, for the light of the sun can only make things clear to the eyes, but the light that the Prophet brings to the world makes the heart see all that the eyes are not capable of seeing. The Prophet brings Love—the Love of God, the Father and Mother of the whole humanity: a Love that is Life itself. No words or actions can express that Love. The presence of the Prophet, his very being, speaks of it, if only the heart had ears to listen. Verily, to the believer all is right, and to the unbeliever all is wrong.

The principal work of the Prophet is to glorify the Name of God, and to raise humanity from the denseness of the earth, to open the doors of the human heart to the divine beauty which is everywhere manifested, and to illuminate souls which are groping in darkness for years. The Prophet brings the Message of the day, a reform for that particular period in which he is born. A claim of a prophet is nothing to the real Prophet. The being of the Prophet, the work of the Prophet, and the fulfillment of his task, is itself the proof of prophethood.

The Spirit of Guidance

The *Spirit of Guidance* in other words may be called the *Divine Mind*; and as the human mind is finished after its coming on earth, so the Divine Mind becomes completed after manifestation. Plainly speaking, the Creator's Mind is made of His own creation. The experience of every soul becomes the experience of the Divine Mind; therefore, the Divine Mind has the knowledge of all beings. It is a storehouse of perfect wisdom. It is the Soul of Christ, and the Spirit of prophecy. Intuition, inspiration, vision, or revelation, all have the Divine Mind as the. Source from whence every kind of revelation comes.

There are some who receive the knowledge from the Divine Mind indirectly, and some receive it directly. Souls who happen to receive the central current of the Spirit of Guidance, in such souls the spirit of prophecy is conceived. The Messengers of all times, of whom we hear in the histories and traditions of the world, have been souls in whom the central current of the Divine Light has functioned. In other words, the Prophets of all ages have been the reflections of the Divine Mind on earth. No one has ever seen God, and if the evidence of God has ever been manifested, it was in man who reflected God. Besides all the Prophets have taught, it was the personality of the Prophets which proved their prophecy. In their thought, speech, and word they reflected God, which was more than morals, doctrines, and teachings could do.

Every inspired person reflects in his own way some divine spark hidden in his soul, which wins the world. A musician may show his inspiration in music; a poet may show it in his poetry; an artist may show his inspiration in his art; but the central ray of light which the Prophets reflect, falling upon every plane and every aspect of life, makes all things clear to their sight. Therefore their presence clears away perplexity from the minds of the confused ones. A person in the presence of the Prophet can feel and think more clearly, even without having spoken to the Prophet. Many forget their questions when before a Prophet, for the light, falling upon their hearts, brings them the answer, and they find out that the answer was in themselves, something that they had already known. No doubt it is true that the question and answer both are in the soul. The first step of the soul's progress raises questions, and the second step is the answer. It is, therefore, that a prophetic soul is a physician at the same time; a prophetic soul is a scientist, an artist, is capable of commerce, industry, and business, qualified in warfare and competent in peacemaking:

The Spirit of Guidance is as the yeast which is used to make bread, to prepare humanity for the purpose for which it was created. The Spirit of Guidance is a plant that grows and blossoms when it receives response and care; and when it is watered by the rainfall of divine inspiration it blooms in the light of the Divine Sun. The Spirit of Guidance is the Light of God, which may be likened to a lantern that the farmer carries when walking on the farm in the darkness of night. The Spirit of Guidance is like a searchlight. Any object on which the searchlight is thrown, it shows clearly; so the Spirit of Guidance thrown upon any aspect of life gives one a keen insight into it. In the Spirit of Guidance one finds a living God active in the heart of every person.

One who depends upon the Spirit of Guidance to guide his life is guided aright. We always have a counsel within, but the one who ignores the existence of such a thing as the Spirit of Guidance is left alone for some time by the Spirit of Guidance to look out for himself. It is like the mother and the dependent child, who tries to hold the hand of the mother at every step it takes; so the mother's whole attention is drawn to every step of her child. But when the child tries to move about by his own will, and tries to keep away, then the attention of the mother, to some extent, becomes released. This does not mean that the mother gives up entirely the care of the child; it only means that the mother allows the child to have its awn way to some extent, and feels sorry when the child falls and hurts itself. In point of fact, all souls are children of God, but such souls as are conscious of their relation to God, as between a child and his parents, certainly deserve to be called the children of God. They are especially cared for; they are always guided; because they ask for guidance.

The soul of the Prophet, therefore, shows the innocence of the child. Of what is known about Jesus Christ and His life to the world, the most lovable attribute of the Master was His innocence in spite of His perfect wisdom. Certainly He deserves to be called the Only-Begotten Son Who has all His life depended for everything He said or did upon the guidance from God.

The Form of the Message

This is a question which is always asked: how the prophetic soul receives the Message of God: in what form? Does the Angel Gabriel bring this, as it is said in the scriptures of Beni Israel? Does it come as a voice? Does it come in a form which is visible? And the answer is that everything which has been said in the ancient scriptures regarding it has so much truth in it, though very often some symbolical ideas are misinterpreted by the uninitiated. Gabriel as a Messenger is, in part, imagination. The real Gabriel is that Spirit of Guidance which is the soul of the Prophets. Its voice is intuition, but to the attentive mind of the Prophet sometimes this voice is so distinct that it becomes much louder than what one hears through the ears. For in their hearts a capacity is produced; in other words, their hearts become as domes which give echo to every word. The heart of the ordinary person does not give that echo; so the inner voice becomes inaudible to one's own soul. As a voice is necessary, so hearing is necessary also; without the hearing the voice is inaudible. The hearing is the capacity in the heart. When the heart becomes as an ear, then it begins to hear the voice that comes from within.

And now the question comes whether a Gabriel manifested to the Prophets in a certain form. That is true also. There is nothing in this world which is void of form, except God, Who is formless. The form of some things is visible, and of other things invisible. Even thoughts and feelings have forms. You may call them results, but form is always a result. The heart which can hear the inner voice louder than the spoken words can certainly see the form, even the form which is not seen by every soul. The question: "Do the eyes of the Prophet see a form?"—may be answered: "Yes." For what the heart sees fully, that becomes reflected in the eyes also. It is not seen from without, but from within, and yet it is seen. Every person cannot conceive of such an idea as this: one who is accustomed to see and hear all that comes from outside. But it is as clear as the day for the wise to know that the eyes and the ears are not only the organs in which the impressions from the outer life are reflected, but even the impressions from the life within are also reflected in them.

It matters little to a Prophet whether his ears hear or his heart hears, whether his eyes see or his heart sees. He knows that he hears and sees, and that is sufficient evidence for him of a living God. One may ask: do you mean by this that God is so personal as to speak and manifest as a phantom to a certain soul? If it were so, it would be nothing but limiting God! In answer to this, I would say that the limitless God cannot be made more intelligible to our limited self unless He was first made limited. That limited ideal becomes as an instrument, as a medium of God Who is perfect and Who is limitless.

The Nature of the
Prophetic Soul

We find in the traditions of the ancients that there were many among the Prophets of the past who, in a worldly sense, were not educated, among them the Prophet Muhammad, who was given the name *Ummi*, by which many called him, which means "unlettered"; although, according to the idea of that time, the Prophet was very well-versed in the Arabic language. This shows that worldly education does not make the Prophet. No doubt it helps to express the spiritual Message which his heart receives in a more intelligible form.

We see in the world's scriptures four different forms in which the prophetic Message was given: the ancient Hindu form, which can be traced in the scriptures of India and which was continued by Buddha; then the form of Beni Israel, which is to be found in the Old Testament, from the time of Abraham to the time of Muhammad; the third form is the form of Zarathustra, which shows two aspects—the one aspect is the *Gayatri* of the Hindus and the other aspect is the prayer of Beni Israel; and the fourth form is the form of the New Testament, which gives the legend and interpretation of the teaching of Jesus Christ, and which was made, at every new version, more intelligible to the mind of the people in the West. But the moment a soul dives deeper into these scriptures it begins to realize the One Voice within all these outer forms, and that it is the same Voice that has adopted these different forms, to answer the need of every age.

What the Prophet says is much less than what he really hears, and the sense of what he says is much deeper than what his outer words mean. For the work of the Prophet is a most difficult one; it is trying to present to the world the whole ocean in a bottle. No one has ever been able to do it; yet They have all tried, for that has been their destiny. People have taken these bottles given to them, and have, said, "See, here is the ocean; I have the ocean in my pocket!" But, by what the Prophets have taught in the scriptures, they have only tried to point out the way; but they have not pictured the Goal, for no one can put the Goal into a picture. The Goal is above all form and beyond the power of words to explain.

Those who have benefited by the life and the Message of the Divine Message Bearers are not necessarily the followers of their Message, but the imitators of their life; for they have not followed the teaching only, but followed the Teacher, who is the living example of his teaching. All the ancient traditions of the religious evolution tell us how those around the Prophets have benefited by the imitation, rather than by following the strict laws and by arguing upon the differences between the laws. There is no scripture in which contradiction does not exist. It is the contradiction which makes the music of the Message. The Message would be rigid, like pebbles, if there were no contradiction. Even all pebbles are not alike; how can all words mean the same? The Message is nothing but an answer to every question, every need, every demand of the individual and collective life. Rumi has tried to explain in the *Masnavi*, from the beginning to the end, the nature and character of the heart of the Prophet, and by this he has given the key to the door which opens to the prophetic path. Therefore in reading any scripture we must remember first that it is not the words we read which are so important as what is hidden behind. To the ordinary mind, that only sees on the surface, the words of the scriptures are nothing but simple phrases, and sometimes the ideas appear simple, even childish. But the one who tries to know what is behind them will find out in time that there is a vast field of thought hidden behind every word that has come from the lips of the Prophets. Verily the words of the Prophets are as seals upon the Secret of God.

The soul of the Prophet represents both the human and the divine. His feet on the earth and his head in heaven, he has to journey on the path of life, to respect and regard reason, and yet to cling to that rope which hangs down from heaven, which he calls faith—one thing contrary to the other. The world of variety, with its numberless changes, compels him to reason out things, and the world of unity promises to his unwavering faith the answer to every demand of life. In the Sufi terms there is a word called *Akhlak-i Allah*, which means "the Manner of God." This Manner is seen in the prophetic soul. For no one knows the Manner of God, as God is not seen by all; and if there is any sign of God seen, it is in the God-conscious one; and it is the fullness of God-consciousness which makes a prophetic soul.

The life of the Prophet is like that of someone walking upon a wire—matter on one side and spirit on the other, heaven on one side and earth on the other—with the imperfect self journeying towards perfection and at the same time holding upon itself the burden of numberless souls, many among whom have not yet learnt to walk even upon the earth. In the history of the Prophets, in whatever time they have come on earth, one reads of their struggle being fourfold: struggle with self, struggle with the world, struggle with friends, and struggle with foes; and yet many wonder, why should a Prophet be a warrior? Many know of the Prophet Muhammad being a warrior, but are ignorant of the fact that Moses had the same experience. And very few know the lives of the Prophets of India, Rama and Krishna, whose whole lives were nothing but warfare from the beginning to the end. Their scriptures are full of the wars and battles through all their lives, and if some apparently did not have a war, they had some other form of warfare to go through. The blood of the martyrs was the foundation of the church.

The Seers and Saints, who live a life of seclusion, are happy when compared to the life of the Prophet, whose life's work is in the midst of the crowd. When he is known to be a Prophet, jealousy and prejudice arise; if he is not known, he can do but little. When he goes into the world, the world absorbs him; when he thinks of God, God attracts him—one spirit pulled from both sides; and it is this that the picture of the cross signifies. The Prophet, representing God and His Message, is tested and tried and examined by every soul; a thousand searchlights are thrown upon him; and he is not judged under one judge, but numberless judges; every soul is a judge, and has his own law to judge him with. The mystic is free to speak and act; what does he care what people think of him? The Prophet must care what they think of him—not for himself, but for those who follow him.

Besides all difficulties, in the end he finds no comprehension of his ideal or service in the world, except in God, Who alone is his consolation. Many follow the Prophet, but very few comprehend his ideal. It is this that made Muhammad say, "I am knowledge; Ali is the door." In the first place, to express a high thought in words or action is the most difficult thing, because what is expressed in words and actions is the thought on the surface; to express deep feeling in words and action is, in the same way, difficult. And so is the Message of the Prophet; it is often difficult to be put into words. The best way of following a prophetic Message—which has been known to very few—is to adopt the outlook of the Prophet; for the point of view of every person one can fully understand by seeing from that person's point of view.

The Attunement of the Prophet

What is asked of a Prophet? The prophetic soul must of necessity rise so high that it may hear the Voice of God, and at the same time it must bend so low that it may hear every little whisper of human beings. Every little lack of consideration or regard for all those who wish to call the attention of the Prophets has been noticed and remarked in the lives of the Prophets. It means to live in heaven and to live on the earth at the same time. The heart of the Prophet is meant to be the harp, every string of it to be tuned to its proper pitch, so that God may play upon it His music. And it is that celestial music which is called the Divine Message. It is therefore that all the ancient scriptures were named *Githas*, or *Gathas*, which means the same thing: "music." The Song Celestial of Krishna is called *Bhagavad Gita*, which means the "Song of God"; and the Parsis call their sacred scripture *Gatha*. The Jewish scriptures are chanted when recited; also the Qur'an is recited in the form of singing.

Every musician knows how difficult it is to keep his violin in tune, especially when it is shaken wherever he has to move in the crowd. The heart, therefore, is incomparably more susceptible to get out of tune. It is therefore that the seers and mystics sought solitude, and kept themselves away from the crowd; but the Prophet, by his natural mission, is placed in the midst of the crowd. It is the problem of life in the crowd which he has to solve, and yet not solve it intellectually, as everyone wishes to do, but spiritually, by keeping that instrument, the heart, in proper tune to the Infinite, that he may get the answer for all questions arising at every moment of the day.

It is therefore that even the presence of the Prophet is the answer to every question: without having spoken one word, the Prophet gives the answer; but if a mind, restless and confused, cannot hear it, then that mind receives the answer in words. The answer of the Prophet uproots every question; but the answer always comes from the heart of the Prophet without his even having been asked a question. For the Prophet is only the medium between God and man; therefore the answer is from God. It is not true that the Prophet answers a question because he reads the mind; it is the mind of the one who asks the question that strikes, in the inner plane, the divine bell, which is the heart of the Prophet; and God, hearing the bell, answers. The answer comes in a manner as if words were put into the mouth of the Prophet. The Prophet, therefore, need not think on the question he is asked; it is all automatic, so that the question draws out of him the answer. This rule is not applied only to individuals, but to the multitude. A thousand people listening to a Prophet at the same time, and each having a different question in his mind, the question of every one of them has been answered. So the true character of the sacred scriptures is that even the book answers the question, if a person opens it automatically in order to find out a solution to a certain problem. Imagine, if the book answers, then one could expect more from the Prophet; for the soul of the Prophet is the living book: his heart is the sacred scripture.

What is religion? In the outer sense of the word, a form given to worship God and a law given to a community to live harmoniously.

And what does religion mean in the inner sense of the word? It means a staircase, made for the soul to climb and reach that plane where Truth is realized. Both these aspects of religion may be found in the words and in the soul of the Prophet: his words, the law; his Message, the wisdom; and his being, that peace which is the seeking of every soul. God has never manifested as Himself in this world of variety, where every thing and every being is a divine expression, yet with its limitations. And if the world has been able to believe in God and to recognize God in a being, it is in the godly, it is in the soul which reflects God. With all the arguments for and against the divinity of Christ, no sincere believer in God can deny that God reflects through the Personality of the Master.

The Prophetic Claim

There are two different conceptions of the prophetic soul. One is as among the Hindus, who call the prophetic souls *Avataras*, which means "Godhead." They have also distinguished the characters of their Avataras from their claims: some claimed to be the Avatar, or the incarnation, of Vishnu; some claimed to be the incarnation of Shiva. It was easy for the people of India to grasp the idea of a Prophet being a God incarnate, rather than to accept a Prophet to be as every other being. Among the Beni Israel, the long line of Prophets was not called incarnations; they were only called the godly, or the ones who were connected with God. And if there are any distinctions, four such distinctions are known. Abraham was called *Habib Allah*, the Friend of God; Moses was distinguished as *Kalim Allah*, a Communicator with God; Jesus was called *Ruh Allah*, the Spirit of God; Muhammad was called *Rasul Allah*, the Messenger of God.

The difference between the Prophets among the Hindus and among the Beni Israel that can be noticed, is one: the Hindu Prophets claim to be God themselves. The reason was that the people in India, owing to their philosophical evolution, were ready to accept the divine in man; but, on the contrary, in Arabia and Palestine even the prophetic claim aroused such opposition against the Prophets that their lives were in danger and their mission became most difficult for them to perform.

After the claimants of Godhead there have been many reformers in India, to whom people responded without much difficulty, but in the Near East it has always been difficult, and will always be so. It is for this reason that the ancient school of esotericism, the ancient Order of the Sufis, found it difficult to exist under the reign of orthodoxy. The lives of many great Sufis have been made victims of the orthodox powers which reigned. Sufism, therefore, which was as a mother of the coming reform in the religious world, was protected by Persia, and, in the end, found a greater freedom in the land of India, where the Hindus respected it and Muslims followed it without the slightest hesitation. In the houses of the Sufis the followers of all religions met together in friendliness and in the feeling of brotherhood.

The Sufi Message which is now being given in the Western world is the child of that mother who has been known for many years as Sufism. The Sufi Message which is being given to the world just now, therefore, connects the two lines of the prophetic mission, the Hindu line and that of Beni Israel, in order that they may become the medium to unite in God and Truth both parts of the world, East and West. It is the same Truth, the same religion, the same ideal, which the wise of all ages have held. If there is anything different, it is only the difference of the form. The Sufi Message given now has adopted the form suitable for the age. It is a Message without claim; and the group of workers in this Message, and those who follow it, are named the Sufi Movement, whose work it is to tread the spiritual path quietly, unassumingly, and to serve God and humanity, in which is the fulfillment of the Message.

Prophets and Religions

Rama

Rama, the great Prophet and ideal of the Hindus, was at the same time the example of Godhead. The character of Rama is said to have been foretold by Valmiki; at the same time, the training which was given to Rama by a great Rishi whose name was Vashishta was a training to bring out that Kingdom of God which is hidden in the heart of man. In this respect Rama was not only an ideal for the Hindus of that particular age, but was a model to mold the character of those who tread the spiritual path in any age.

Rama was a prince by birth, but was given to be trained by a Sage, where he lived the life in the solitude, the life of study and play both together. He was not only taught to read and write, but he was trained in athletic exercises, in sports, and had a training in all the manner of warfare. This shows what education the ancient people had, an education in all directions of life. And, being trained thus, Rama completed his course of study about the time of the prime of his youth.

The story of Rama has been always considered as the most sacred scripture for the Hindus. It is called *Ramayana*. The Brahman recites this story in a poetic form, to which the devotees of the Master listen for hours without being tired of it. For they take it as their religious training.

The most interesting part of Rama's life is his marriage. In the ancient times there was a custom that the husband was chosen. This custom came owing to the tendency to warfare. At every little trouble the princes of the time were up in arms even in such matters as marriage. In order to avoid war, the father of Sita invited all the princes and potentates of his land and gave the right of selection to his daughter. There was a time appointed, when they all gathered in the royal gallery, adorned in their regal ornaments and decorations.

Rama lived a simple life; he had not yet known what princely life means, for he was being trained under a Saint, where he ate the same food as the Sage did, wore the same simple clothes as the Sage, and lived in the woods in the solitude. Yet the brightness of the soul shines out even without ornaments. When Sita entered this assembly, with a garland of flowers in her hands, her first glance fell upon Rama, and she could not lift her glance from that ideal of her soul to anyone else, for her soul recognized the pearl in its heart. Sita, without a moment's pause, came immediately and put the garland on the neck of that youth, so simple and unassuming, standing with an innocent expression behind all the shining hosts. Many marveled at this choice, but many more became as glowing fire with the thought of envy and jealousy. Among them, the one who was most troubled was the King of Lanka, Ravana. For Sita was not only known as the most beautiful princess of the time, but also was called Padmani, the Ideal Maiden. As Rama was an example in his character, so in Sita the ideal character was born.

Then came the separation of the two. Sita, who had followed Rama in his twelve years' *Vanavasa*, which means roaming in the forest, was once left alone in the woods, and Rama had gone to fetch some water. At that time Sita disappeared, and after a great difficulty and a great grief the trace was found. She had been taken prisoner by Ravana. She steadily lived for Rama in this captivity, and would not yield to Ravana's temptations and threatenings. In the end victory was won. Rama fought a battle with Ravana and brought Sita back home.

This story gives the picture of life being a struggle for everyone, in a small way or in a big way. The outer nature of the struggle may be different for everyone, but, at the same time, no one can live in the midst of this world and be without a struggle. In this struggle the one who wins in the end has fulfilled the purpose of his life; who loses in the end, has lost.

The life of Rama suggests that, spiritual strife apart, the struggle in the world is the first thing to face; and if one keeps to one's own ideal through every test and trial in life, one will no doubt arrive at a stage when he will be victorious. It does not matter how small be the struggle, but victory won in the end of every struggle is the power that leads man farther on the path towards life's goal. The life of man, however great and spiritual, has its limitations. Before conditions of life the greatest man on earth, the most powerful soul, will for a moment seem helpless. But it is not the beginning that counts; it is the end. It is the last note that a great soul strikes which proves that soul to be real and true.

Forms of Hindu Worship

The Hindu religion is one of the most ancient religions in the world, and to this almost all religions of the past may be traced. The world's primitive religion, sun worship, which came and went in the world, still exists among the Brahmans. They greet the sunrise after bathing in the river; and they are purified by its most inspiring rays. Besides the sun, they worship the moon and the planets, counting every one of them as a peculiar god, signifying a particular power of God.

The mythical religion of the ancient Greeks, the gods and god-desses of the old Egyptians—all that is found today in the religion of the Hindus. They have among their gods almost all animals and birds known to man; and all different aspects of life are explained in their myths, which teach man to see the Divine Being in all. The great powers of the Almighty are pictured as various gods and god-desses, attributed with special powers. Some worship these. Even such savage animals as lions, elephants, or cobras are considered sacred. By this the moral is taught, to love our enemies.

The fire worship of the Zoroastrians may be seen in the *Yag* and *Yagna* ceremonies of the Hindus. The idea of Trinity of the Christians may be traced in the idea of *Trimurti* in the Hindu religion. The prostration at the prayers, which exists in Islam, may be seen in its complete form in the *Pranam* and *Dandavat* forms of Hindu worship.

Besides all these objects of worship, they are taught the worship of the Guru, the Teacher. The first Guru they see in the mother and father; then every person with whom they come in contact, who teaches them anything, they esteem as their Guru, until they have developed in themselves the worshipful attitude, which in the end they show to the real Guru, who helps them in their spiritual awakening. The following verse, from the Hindi, gives an idea of what the chela thinks of his Guru:

> *I have enjoyed my life on earth, O Guru, by thy mercy.*
> *Thy words have drawn me closer to God.*
> *As with the rising of the sun darkness disappears,*
> *So thou hast cleared away the darkness of ignorance from my soul.*
> *Some adore the earthly beings and some adore the heavenly,*
> *But I revere thee, O holy Guru!*

> (Sundar Das)

The Basis of the Caste System among Hindus

When the Aryans came and settled in Bharat Khand, which is today called India, they wanted to make the life there a life of solitude and self-sufficiency.

Those among them who were learned and pious, whose living was better in every way than the others', grouped themselves, and called themselves *Brahmans*, whose part of work was study, scientific investigation, music, poetry; and priesthood was their right. They taught people as teachers. At the wedding ceremonies and at births and deaths they took charge of the ceremonies with their religious rite. Their life was as the life of a hermit. The difference was that they married among their own people. Their living only depended upon *Bhiksha* — free will offerings.

There were others among them who revered the Brahmans for their learning and piety, but held themselves superior for their warlike merits and for their control of the land that belonged to them. They were called *Kshattriya* (landowners, or warriors).

Those who were clever at commerce took refuge under the power and control of the Kshattriya, and took in their hands all concerning money. They were called *Vaishyas*. Business of all kinds was carried on by them.

Those remaining were the ones who labored, and, according to their labor, among them grades were formed. They were called *Shudras*. Among them were some whose work was of such a nature that their coming in the house, or touching another person when working, would be against the sanitary law. Brahmanism being the most scientific religion, it made a law that they should not be touched.

In this way these four castes were formed, and went on peacefully until the entry of foreigners into their land, which naturally interfered with their harmony, and the whole plan became a failure.

With all the wisdom in forming these four castes, there is a self-ishness shown on the part of the high classes, as has been always the case with the human race; and that has been a great hindrance to the progress of Hindus in general, for every chance of progress was shut out for the lower classes. Their only consolation was to reincarnate and be born in a higher class. If not, there was no other way. This is the chief reason which gave the doctrine of reincarnation importance in the Hindu race.

Krishna

The life of Krishna is an ideal which gives the picture of the life of a perfect man. The real meaning of the word *Krishna* is God, and the man who was identified with that name was the God-conscious one who fulfilled His Message in the period in which he was destined to give His Message.

The story of Krishna, apart from its historical value and interest, is of great importance to the seeker after Truth. No one knows of the father and mother of Krishna. Some say he was of royal birth. It means of kingly origin, from that King Who is the King of all. Then he was given in the care of Yeshoda, who brought him up as his guardian mother. This is symbolical of the earthly parents, who are the guardians, the real father and mother being God. In the childhood of Krishna, it is said, he was fond of butter, and he learned, as a child, to steal butter from everywhere. And the meaning is, that wisdom is the butter of the whole life. When life is churned through a wheel, then out of that comes butter; wisdom is gained by it. He was stealing it; which means, wherever he found wisdom he learned it, from everybody's experience he benefited— that is stealing.

Plainly speaking, there are two ways of learning wisdom. The one way of learning wisdom is that a person goes and drinks to excess, and then falls down in the mud, and then the police take

him to the police station, and when he recovers from his drunken-
ness he cannot find his clothes and he is horrified at his own
appearance. This makes him realize what he has done. This is one
way of learning, and it is possible that he does not learn. The other
way of learning is that a young man is going along the street; he
sees a drunken man, and sees how terrible it is to be in this position;
he learns from that. That is stealing the butter.

But then the latter part of Krishna's life has two very important
aspects. One aspect teaches us that life is a continual battle, and the
earth is the battlefield where every soul has to struggle, and the one
who will own the kingdom of the earth must know very well the law
of warfare. The secret of the offensive, the mystery of defense, how
to hold our position, how to retreat, how to advance, how to
change position, how to protect and control all that has been won,
how to let go what must be given up, the manner of sending an
ultimatum, the way of making an armistice, the method by which
peace is made—all this is to be learned. In this life's battle man's
position is most difficult, for he has to fight on two fronts at the
same time: one is himself, and the other is before him. If he is suc-
cessful on one front, and on the other front he proves to have failed,
then his success is not complete.

And the battle of each individual has a different character. The
battle depends upon man's particular grade of evolution. Therefore
every person's battle in life is different, of a peculiar character. And
no person in the world is free from that battle; only one is more
prepared for it; the other, perhaps, is ignorant of the law of warfare.
And in the success of this battle there is the fulfillment of life. The
Bhagavad Gita, the Song Celestial, from the beginning to the end,
is a teaching on the law of life's warfare.

The other outlook of Krishna on life is that every soul is striving to attain God, but God, not as a Judge or a King, but as a

Beloved. And every soul seeks God, the God of Love, in the form it is capable of imagining. And in this way the story of Krishna and the gopis signifies God and the various souls seeking perfection.

The life and teaching of Krishna have helped the people of India very much in broadening the thought of the pious. The religious man, full of dogmas, is often apt to make dogmas too rigid, and expects the godly, or the God-conscious, to fit in with his standard of goodness. If they do not fit in with his particular idea of piety he is ready to criticize them. But the thought and life of Krishna were used by the artist and the poet and the musician, and out of it was made a new religion, a religion of recognizing the divine in natural human life. And that idea of considering a spiritual person exclusive, remote, stone-like, and lifeless ceased to exist. The people of India became much more tolerant toward all different aspects of life, looking at the whole life, at the same time, as an Immanence of God.

The Worshipers of Krishna

Among Hindus some are called by this name; for all Hindus belong to one religion, and yet there are different gods and goddesses worshiped by different people among Hindus. The worship of Krishna is most prevalent among them, and it is as ceremonial as the ancient Church of Rome, and even more so. This teaches us that ceremony is a concrete expression of thought, and it has suited the masses better than a religion of thought alone.

In the temple of Krishna there is an image of Krishna lying in a cradle. Women who go there for worship will sing lullabies in a prayerful attitude. Then there is an image in the same temple of Krishna grown up; and with him the image of Radha, his consort. Men and women will go there and worship both. They will take flowers and sandalwood and a few grains of rice in order to make an offering to the god. Then there is an image of Krishna with a sword, cutting off the head of Kounsa, the monster. Then there are engravings in the temple of Krishna driving the chariot of Arjuna, the exiled King of India, when going to wage war against the Pandavas, the rulers of the time.

At first sight it surprises a stranger to think that God is worshiped in the man's form, and God is considered so small as to be rocked in a cradle, and to picture God Most High standing with his wife, and then to see God going to war, which any kindhearted person would refuse to do. But to a Sufi it gives a different impression, since he sees God in every form. First, he says that if the worshiper cultivates his patience by standing, in his joy and trouble, before a heedless god of stone that never answers or stretches out a helping hand, he can only be a steady worshiper of the true God, and will not fail, as many do when they have no help given by God, who then begin to disbelieve, or at least to doubt His existence. He thinks that when He is all and in all, what does it matter if one looks at heaven and the other looks at earth? To his mind both are looking at the same thing.

In ancient times many had thought that spirituality means to be alone in a forest, which thought is broken by seeing Krishna and Radha both, which means that both mean God, not one alone.

Many today question: "If there is God, why should wars and disasters take place?" And many give up their belief when they think more about it. The image of Krishna with a sword and going to war shows that it is God Who is in heaven, it is God Who is most kind, but it is the same God Who stands with a sword; that there is no name, no form, no place, no occupation, which is void of God. It is a lesson to recognize God in all, instead of limiting God only to the good and keeping Him away from what we call evil, which goes against the saying that "in God we live and move and have our being."

Buddha

India, a land of extremes, was once very much engrossed in idealism. Idealism gave to the people Brahmanism, an idealism which had reached its greatest heights, an idealism which made them recognize the Face of God in man, and to experience heaven on earth. And when this touched its zenith, then came another epoch, an epoch of reaction, and that was the period of Buddha. The mission of Buddha was quite peculiar in its character, and therefore it stands quite different from the many different religions of the world. And people sometimes wonder if all religions are one. They can quite well see a similarity between the Hebrew religion and Islam, also the religion of the Christ; but they cannot understand that there could be a religion of Buddha, and that it could be also a religion, and that it could be one with all others. And the answer is this: that the work of all those who have served humanity in the form of religion has been of great importance—for the first reason, that they had to give the same Truth which every other Server of humanity has given; and for the next reason, that they had to answer the demand of the time in a form suited for that particular time; and in that they differed from their predecessors, who had done the work in other ways. It may not be forgotten that among Hindus idealism had reached its zenith, and it did not remain for Buddha to teach a greater idealism than they already had. In order, therefore, to bring about a balance, he had to give a pill of disillusion. And in that way perhaps at that time, or even today, he might appear to be a teacher of quite a different philosophy and a religion which is different from all other religions, which are of idealism. And at the same time no one can show one word in the teaching of Buddha where Buddha has opposed any religion. Only his mission was to bring the birds of idealism, flying in the air, nearer to the earth, because the food of their body belonged to the earth.

Buddha, born as a prince, was recognized by the wise of that time as a soul which had the finest feeling that it could have, and the deepest depth in his heart. Being born in a family where he could be taken good care of, naturally they closed all the sorrows and distress and troubles of life away from him, and kept him in a surrounding where no sorrows, distress, and troubles of life could touch him, in order to give this soul the time to develop, without being depressed by worldly troubles. It was not only the love of the parents, but it was the wisdom of destiny, that brought him up in this manner, a soul who was born to sympathize with the world. And when the mind of Buddha, after the best education that he received, came to maturity, then he was one day allowed to go out and look at the world. This soul, who was not allowed to see much of the world and who had not known pain and distress and trouble, was quite unaware of the experience that the life in the world shows to man. Then he went out for the first time; he looked at a person who was aged and only with difficulty could walk. And he said, "What is it?" They said, "It is age." And he sympathized. And then he saw another person, worn out and tired and downhearted. And he said, "What is the matter?" And they said, "It is illness." And he sympathized, and said, "There is such a thing as illness." There was another person who had lost his money and was in a great despair, and was in poverty. Buddha asked, "What is it?" They said, "It is poverty." And he sympathized, and he felt his condition. In short, this soul, whose heart was open to sympathize with everyone, felt that life has many limitations and every limitation has its despair. And the number of limitations that he saw was so great that he thought what must be the remedy for all these limitations.

In the first place he saw that human nature seeks for happiness. It is not because happiness is outside of man; it is because happiness belongs to him. Then he saw that all these limitations make a barrier for man, thereby depriving him of the consciousness of this happiness which is his own. He also saw that all the manner of distress, and all the causes of distress, if they were removed, still man would not be free from distress, because the nature of man is to find happiness; he is not looking for distress. For no one in the world is seeking for a distress, and almost everyone in the world finds distress without seeking for it. He saw that the removing of these apparent limitations was not sufficient, but it is the study of life, observation, analysis, that is the most necessary. He found in the end that it is the analysis of life, a thorough analysis, which clears one's reason from all darkness, and produces in it its own original light. Man is distressed by looking at the distress without having studied it. That is generally the case. Every distress that comes to man he is afraid of, and he partakes of it without first having faced it and studied it analytically. But at the same time Buddha saw that if there was a key to happiness, it came by throwing analytical light upon all the different situations of life. This Buddha taught in the form of religion more than two thousand years ago. And today the reasoning that is looking for a solution in the modern world is now finding the same solution which Buddha found over two thousand years ago; and they call it psychoanalysis.

It is the beginning of that something which had reached to its highest top, and this analysis in itself had reached to the highest idealism.

Buddha was the title of Gautama. He was called Buddha because his spirit expressed the meaning of the word *Buddh*. The word *Buddh* in Sanskrit means "reason." In the Buddhistic terminology the Spirit of Guidance is named *Bodhisattva*, which means the essence of reason. Reason in its essence is of a liquid form: it is the cream of intelligence. When it is crystallized, it becomes rigid. Very often intellectuality explains a knowledge formed by reasons, most of them of rigid character. The fine reason is subtle; the finer the reason, the less it can be explained in words. It is therefore that people with fine reason cannot very well put their reason into words. Reason in its essence is the depth of intelligence. The intelligence knows, not because it has learned; it knows because it knows. In this higher reason the Spirit of Guidance is conceived, and from that fountain of reason all the great Prophets have drunk.

In the teaching of true Buddhism, Buddha has never been considered as an exclusive personality. Buddha has been known to the Buddhists who have understood his Message rightly as a man who attained the realization of that essence of reason in which is the fulfillment of life's purpose.

Worshiping Buddha does not mean that the Buddhist worships the personality of his spiritual Master. He only means by this worship that if there is any object that deserves worship most, it is a human being; it is the person from whose heart the essence of reason, *Buddhi,* has risen as a spring. By this knowledge he recognizes the possibility for every soul, whatever be his grade of evolution, of attaining that bliss, trusting that the innermost being of every soul is divine.

The honey of life is hope. If the knowledge of God does not give hope to attain the divine bliss which is attained in life, that knowledge is of no use. Man may believe in God for years and yet may not be benefited by the spiritual bliss; for the spiritual bliss is not only in *believing*, but it is in *knowing* God.

Buddhi, which is subtle reasoning, is the path which leads to the goal. The absence of that keeps a person in obscurity. As the sun is the source of light, which shows outwardly things in life, so *Buddhi* is the inner source of light, which enables the person to see life clearly, inwardly and outwardly. The true aim of the disciples of Buddha has not been only to adhere to Buddha, his name or his ideal, but, by taking Buddha as an example before him, their idea was to become Buddha some day. And the same idea is the secret of Sufism.

Forms of Buddhistic Worship

Buddhism is so named from Buddha; yet the meaning of the word denotes the knower, the seer, the word *Buddhi* in Sanskrit being the name of the faculty in man which knows, which sees, and thereby distinguishes and discriminates between things and beings. It is doubtful if Buddha taught his followers to worship his own image, as they do today. In every temple of the Buddhists, and in their monasteries, the statues of Buddha, of all sizes, in gold, silver, brass, and copper, are found, where Buddha is sitting cross-legged in the mystic posture. No home of a Buddhist, no sacred place, is without his statue. And though the four important scriptures of the Buddhistic faith are lost, and have vanished long ago, still the fragrance of his philosophy and moral could not be lost sight of. Although it seems to be idolatry, yet his image, as a symbol, inspires not only his devotees, but every thoughtful mind, as it shows balance, quietude, peace, the absorption within, purity of character, beauty of personality, gentleness, tenderness, a restful attitude, and perfect wisdom.

As today in the modern civilized countries the statues of heroes, royalties, commanders of armies, politicians, poets, writers, and musicians are found exposed everywhere, and the Statue of Liberty reminds America of national freedom, so to a Buddhist the statue of Buddha speaks of spiritual liberation. Why should it be regarded as any worse if the Buddhists have the statue of their Inspirer between them, whose very image elevates their soul toward the highest ideals, and the life of renunciation and self-denial that their Teacher led?

Buddhism, being the rival and the child of Brahmanism, could not very well leave out the influence of its parent religion. Although Buddhism denies belief in all that is unproven by logic, such as God, soul, meditation, or hereafter, yet the image worship of the Brahmans still exists among Buddhists in the worship of Buddha, and belief in reincarnation and the law of karma may be found inherent among the Buddhists.

Jainism

Jainism is a religion vastly spread in India, the germ of which can be found in Buddhism. This aspect of Buddhism is most admirable, especially in its teaching, "Harmlessness is the only religion." The Jains are vegetarians, but, besides that, they do not harm even the smallest life. Many among them guard themselves against causing harm even to beetles, mosquitoes, ants, bees, scorpions, and snakes, which are so often found in a tropical country.

Their whole moral is based upon the principle of harmlessness, and their priests cause still less harm than the other followers of Jainism. In order to be least harmful, they avoid wearing shoes, avoiding two harms thereby: one being that the leather which is used to make shoes causes the death of so many lives, and the other that by walking with shoes one crushes and kills more lives than by walking barefoot. Some among them are seen with a little piece of cloth tied over their lips, for by walking with open mouth, as so many do, so many small lives are drawn into the mouth. Also there is another reason, that is, to keep as much as possible from talking. Mostly inharmony and a great many other faults are caused by talkativeness, which is often needless.

Abraham

Abraham, whose name seems to come from the Sanskrit root *Brahm*, which means "the Creator," was the father of three great religions of the world. For it is from his descendants, who were called Beni Israel, that came Judaism, Christianity, and Islam.

Abraham was the first to bring the knowledge of mysticism from Egypt, where he was initiated in the most ancient Order of esotericism. And the place which, on his return, he chose to establish as a center, with the idea that some place must be the world center, was Mecca, whither not only in the age of Islam did people make pilgrimage, but at all times the sacred center of Mecca was held in esteem by the pious who lived before Muhammad.

The family of Jesus Christ is traced in the ancient tradition from the family of Isaac, and Muhammad came from the family of Ishmael. The prophecies of Abraham have always been living words, though various people make their different interpretations according to their own ideas. But to the mind of the seer the prophecies of Abraham have a very deep meaning.

With his great knowledge of esotericism, he has been a great patriarch among his people. He was interested in everybody's trouble and difficulty. He was thrown in the midst of worldly responsibilities, to learn all that he might learn from it, and then to teach his knowledge and experience to those who looked to him for the bread of knowledge. No doubt the stories of the ancient times very often strike our modern ears as most childish. But it is the way they were told, and the kind of people that told them; all that makes a great difference. In the first place, there was such a scarcity of lettered people in those days; therefore, the stories were told by the unlettered, and certainly they must have improvised upon every legend they told, and pictured it according to the artistic development of their particular age. Nevertheless, Truth is there, if we only knew how to lift the veil.

Abraham's life does not only make him a Prophet, but a Murshid at the same time. He was a mystic; he gave counsel to those who came to him in need. He examined them, treated their minds, healed their souls according to their needs. The most remarkable thing one notices in Abraham is that, besides being a Prophet and a mystic, he lived the life of an ordinary human being, one with his fellow men in their times of pleasure and sorrow.

One story of the life of Abraham has been the source of great argument in the East, which is the sacrifice of Isaac. It is not only an argument in the East, but alarming to a Western mind. They can put a thousand questions to give a proper reason and justification to such an act. But at the same time, if we looked from the ideal point of view, no sacrifice for a beloved ideal can be too great. There are numberless souls whose dear ones, their beloved husbands or sons, have been sacrificed in this recent war. They could do nothing else; they had to surrender their will to the ideal of the nation, and offer the sacrifice for the cause of the nation, without thinking for one moment that it was unusual. When we think deeply on the problem of life, there is no path in the world, whether spiritual or material, which we can tread successfully without a sacrifice. Sometimes the sacrifice is great, and sometimes small;

sometimes the sacrifice is made first, before achieving the success, and sometimes afterwards. As sacrifice is necessary in life, it is made by everyone in some form or other, but, when it is made willingly, it turns into a virtue. The greater the ideal, the greater the sacrifice it demands, and if one saw wisely the process of advancement through life in any direction, it is nothing but a continual sacrifice. And happiness comes from the understanding of this nature of life, and not being hurt or troubled by it, but knowing that it is by sacrifice, made to the end, that man attains to the desired goal.

The idea of sacrifice has existed in every religion of all ages in some way or another, and has been taught sometimes as having to part with one's possessions for the love of a higher ideal, which means that when man claims to show love for his higher ideal, and yet is not willing to give up something he possesses for it, then there is doubt about his devotion. Although sacrifice of a possession is the first step, the next is self-sacrifice, which was the inner tone of the religion of Jesus Christ. Charity, generosity, even tolerance and forbearance, are a kind of sacrifice, and it seems that every sacrifice in life, in whatever form, means a step forward, which leads to the goal of every soul.

Moses

Moses, the most shining Prophet of the Old Testament, gave to the world the Divine Law, the Ten Commandments, which in reality was the interpretation of the Divine Law that he perceived, expressed in the words of those who stood before him at that time of the world's civilization. It is interesting to notice the Sufi saying which comes from the ages, which says: "Be the follower of love, and forget all distinctions"; for in this path of spiritual attainment to claim that "I am So-and-so" is meaningless. Moses was found by the riverside by a princess, who knew not what family he came from, or who was his father and mother. Only the Name of God came to the mind of every thoughtful inquirer as to the Father and Mother of Moses. When people compare the teachings of different religions, and readily form their opinions upon them, they are often mistaken; it is premature to make such distinctions. There comes a stage in the evolution of an illuminated soul when he begins to see the law hidden behind Nature, the true psychology. To him the whole life reveals the secrets of its nature and character, and when he gives an interpretation of these secrets to others, they become limited, for they take the color of his own personality, and the form of the thought of those to whom the Message is given. The story of Moses, as told by Sufis, is most interesting and helpful to the traveler on the path. Moses has been the favorite character of the poets of Arabia and Persia, and, in the poems of the Persian Sufis, Moses is as often mentioned as Krishna is mentioned in the poetry of the Hindus.

Moses was walking in the wilderness seeking the light when he saw from a distance smoke rising on the top of a mountain. So he climbed to the top of the mountain, in order to find that fire. But on arriving at the top of the mountain he saw a glimpse of the lightning which was so powerful that it went throughout his whole being. Moses fell down unconscious on the ground, and when he recovered his senses, he found himself with illumination. From that time Mount Sinai was the place where he often went and communicated with God. The story is very enlightening when one can think that it is possible, that all the illumination that is desired, can come to a soul in a moment. Many think that spiritual attainment can be achieved by a great labor. No, labor is necessary for material attainment; for spiritual attainment what one needs is the seeking soul like that of Moses. Moses' falling down upon the ground may be interpreted as the Cross, which means: "I am not; Thou art." In order to be, one must pass a stage of being nothing. In the Sufi terms it is called *Fana*, when one thinks "I am not (what I had always thought myself to be)." This is the true self-denial, which the Hindus called *Layam*, and in Buddhism is termed *annihilation*. It is the annihilation of the false self, which gives rise to the true self; once this is done, from that moment man approaches closer and closer to God, and stands face to face with his Divine Ideal, with whom he can communicate at every moment of his life. The law of God is endless, as limitless as God Himself, and, once the eye of the seeker penetrates through the veil that hangs before him, hiding from his eye the real law of life, the mystery of the whole life manifests to him, and happiness and peace become his own, for they are the birthright of every soul.

Zarathustra

The life and teaching of Zarathustra give an example, to those who tread the spiritual path, of the manner in which to begin the spiritual journey. Zarathustra is said to have been born from the Huma-tree. The interpretation of this idea is that the Spirit of Guidance does not come direct from Heaven; he is born from the human family; the tree is the family.

It has been a great error of some religious people that out of their devotion for their Master they placed him, through their imagination, on a pedestal, where they themselves could not ever prove him to be when it came to reasoning. It can only stand in the horizon of faith. No doubt faith is in the foundation. Faith is the lamp which lightens the path, but reason is the globe over it to make its light appear.

The purpose of this whole creation is fulfilled in attaining that perfection which is for a human being to attain. All the Saints, Sages, Prophets, and Masters of Humanity have been human beings, and divine perfection they have shown in fulfilling the purpose of being human.

Zarathustra's spiritual attainment came by his communication with Nature first. He appreciated, adored, and worshiped the sublimity of Nature, and he saw wisdom hidden in the whole creation.

He learned and recognized from that the being of the Creator, acknowledged His perfect wisdom, and then devoted his whole life to glorifying the Name of God. To those who followed him in the path of spiritual attainment, he showed the different aspects of Nature, and asked them to see what they could see behind it all. He pointed out to his followers that the form and line and color and movement that they saw before them, and which attracted them so much, must have been accomplished by an expert artist. It cannot all work mechanically and be perfect. The mechanism, however much perfected, cannot run without the help of an engineer. Therefore he showed to them that God is not an object which the imagination has made, though He is molded by man's imagination outwardly. In reality, God is the Being: such a perfect Being that, if compared with other living beings of this world, He is beyond comparison. He is the Only Being.

The way of worship taught by Zarathustra was to worship God by offering homage to Nature. For Nature suggests to the soul the Endless and Unlimited Being hidden behind it all.

The Zoroastrian Way of Worship

The source of Zoroastrianism is the same as the source of Hinduism, although Hinduism has been practiced in India and the followers of Zoroastrianism have been in Persia. The original source of these sister religions of the Aryans was sun worship. These are the direct descendants of the parent religion of sun worship, though this is the ancestor of the religion of the Hebrew prophets also. No religion can escape from this ancestry.

The Zoroastrians, even today, worship the god Ahura Mazda by looking and bowing to the sun. The symbolical meaning of this is the worship of the light, and especially one Light which has not its like anywhere, which shines upon all things, and by which all things are reflected, and upon which the life of the whole universe absolutely depends. This was the lesson given in ancient times to prepare men's minds to become fond of light, that the soul may unfold some day, and the light from within, the Eternal Sun, the reflection of which on the surface is the sun, may be vouchsafed and be worshiped.

People have called the Zoroastrians fire worshipers. It is a fact. They keep in their place of worship a constantly burning fire, but it is an object they keep before them when thinking of God, as fire purifies all things, and the light within purifies all souls. It is, in fact, a great comfort to have fire in the cold climate, and especially incense burning, which takes away the dampness of the place and gives a facility to the free and deep inhaling and exhaling of breath.

Another thing is that, on earth, it is fire which is the substitute of the sun, for its flame gives light. It is again awakening the mind to the light within.

They worship before the running streams of water and the different scenes of Nature which speak to the hearer of the Divine Immanence in them.

They have in their houses the pictures of Zarathustra, their Prophet, with a torch in his hand, somewhat in the likeness of Christ. The garb is different; it is of old Persia. As the Teacher of every community is pictured in some way, it always inspires those who look at it with that attitude of mind.

The Symbol of Zunar among Zoroastrians

Every Zoroastrian woman or man wears in the vest a cord of silk, and considers it the most sacred thing for its religious significance. This is the custom that has been observed by Zoroastrians from the beginning of their religion, as Zarathustra himself wore this sacred thread, and it is seen till now with Parsis—those that have left Persia, their original land, for ages, and have adopted mostly the customs of India, the land where they took refuge after leaving their country, where a Brahman wears a thread crossways over one shoulder.

This thread they purify with water, fire, and air, and untie and tie it several times during the day, and, every time they do it, they consider it as the most important part of their prayer. It is true that few among them will be found who know the real meaning of this prayer with the thread, but it is mostly so with the followers of different religions.

The moral meaning of *Zunar* is service. A soldier, a policeman, a postman, or a gatekeeper, when on duty, has a belt on, which expresses that he is on duty—not free to do everything he wishes, but only that which he is appointed to his post to accomplish. This explains that man, as the most intelligent of God's creatures, is not supposed to lead his life as he wishes to lead it, but to consider the duty for which he is born and the service that he must render to God and His creatures. As man is apt to forget all that is not to his immediate interest, the loosing and the tying of the thread reminds him of his duty, as the belt reminds the soldier that he is on service. The idea is that we are all servants of God, and we must do all things for Him, Who has created us, supports us, and has engaged us in His service.

But the mystical meaning of *Zunar* is still greater. It makes the vertical figure of man, against the horizontally-worn *Zunar*, a cross. That means, as the Sufi understands, self-denial—"I am not." When that first I, the false I, is so denied, then the next I, which is the real I, awakens, when God Himself realizes His Being, and accomplishes thereby the purpose of creation.

Zoroastrianism

A keen student of the Zoroastrian Scriptures, with illuminated mind, will be able to notice that every invocation that the holy

Zarathustra has used is as if he prayed to the Light within to guide him by all evidences that Nature presented before him; to strengthen the conviction that all is of God, created by God and ruled by God. The mystical meaning of *Ahura Mazda*, upon whom Zarathustra called, is the *Universal Breath*.

Zarathustra has considered three aspects of sin and virtue: *Manashni*, *Gayashni*, and *Kunashni*; thinking, speaking, and doing—that a sin can be committed, not by action alone, but even by intending to commit it, or by saying, "I will do it." And the same is the nature of virtue.

The Teachings of Holy Zarathustra

The chief point in the teachings of holy Zarathustra is the path of goodness; and he separates goodness from badness, calling God the All-good and Satan the All-bad. According to this point of view of the Master, God was, as He is always, the Ideal of worship; and nothing but good can be praised, and none but the good worshiped, and all which is bad naturally leads man astray and veils from his eyes all good. The spirit of evil was personified by the Master, as it had already been personified by the ancients, as Satan.

As the point of view makes all the difference in every teaching, so it made a difference in this teaching of Zoroaster. So that many, instead of taking the true spirit of this idea, have drawn a line between good and bad, and produced, so to speak, two gods: God, the All-good, and Satan, the Lord of Evil. This helped morally to a certain extent but deprived many, who could not catch the real spirit of the Master, of the realization of God, the Only Being. The good God is named by Zoroaster *Ahura Mazda*, the first word meaning literally "indestructible," the next word meaning "supreme God."

Jesus

The Christ spirit is unexplainable in words. The omnipresent intelligence, which is in the rock, in the tree, in the animal, in man shows its gradual unfoldment; it is a fact accepted by both science and metaphysics. This intelligence shows its culmination in the complete development of human personality, in the Personality such as that of Jesus Christ was recognized by his followers to be. The followers of Buddha recognized the same unfoldment of the Object of Creation in Gautama Buddha, and the Hindus saw the same in Sri Krishna. In Moses the followers of Moses recognized that, and maintained their belief for thousands of years. And the same culmination of the all-pervading intelligence was recognized in Muhammad by his followers.

No man has the right to claim this stage of development, nor can anyone very well compare two persons recognized by their followers as the perfect Spirit of God. For a thoughtless person it is easy to express his opinion and to compare two people, but a thoughtful person thinks whether he has arrived at that stage where he can compare two such personalities.

No doubt a question of belief is different. Neither can the belief of the Muslim be the same belief as that of the Jewish people, nor can the Christian belief be the same as that of the Buddhists.

However, the wise man understands all beliefs, for he is one with them all.

And the question if a person was destined to be a complete personality may be answered that there is no person who is not destined to be something. Every person has his life designed beforehand, and the light of the purpose that he is born to accomplish in life has already been kindled in his soul. Therefore, whatever be the grade of a person's evolution, he is certainly destined to be so. Discussion of the lives that the different Prophets have lived, as to the superiority of one over the other, seems to be a primitive attempt on the part of man, who, when not knowing the condition of that particular time when the Prophet lived nor the psychology of the people at the time when the Prophet existed, is ready to judge that personality by the standard of ideas which he knows today, and does not do that personality Justice. And when a person compares one particular teaching of a Prophet with the teaching of another Prophet, he also makes a great mistake, because the teachings of the Prophets have not all been of the same kind. The teachings are like the composition of a composer who writes music in all the different keys, and who puts the highest note and the lowest note and all the notes of different octaves in his music. The teachings of the Prophets are nothing but the answer to the demands of individuals and collective souls. Sometimes a childlike soul comes and asks, and an answer is given appropriate to his understanding; and an old soul comes and asks, and he is given an answer suited to his evolution. When two teachings are brought together, it is not doing justice to compare a teaching which Krishna gave to a child and a teaching which Buddha gave to an old soul. It is easy to say, "I do not like the music of Wagner; I simply hate it." But I should think it would be better to become like Wagner first and then to hate, if one likes. To weigh, to measure, to examine, to pronounce an opinion on a great personality, one must rise to that development first; otherwise the best thing is a respectful attitude. Respect in any form is the way of the wise.

Then there are simple people who hear about miracles, who give all the importance to what they have read, perhaps, in the traditions about the miracles performed by the great souls, but that is the way they limit the greatness of God to a certain miracle. If God is eternal, then His miracle is eternal; it is always there. There is no such thing as unnatural, nor such a thing as impossible. Things seem unnatural because they are unusual; things seem impossible because they are beyond man's limited reason. Life itself is a phenomenon, a miracle. The more one knows about it, the more one lives conscious of the wonderfulness of life, the more one realizes that, if there is any phenomenon or miracle, it is man's birthright. Who has done it? It is man who can do it and who will do it. But what is most essential is not a miracle; the most essential thing is the understanding of life.

The soul who realized, before he claimed to be Alpha and Omega, is Christ. To know intellectually that life is eternal, or that the whole life is one, is not sufficient, although it is the first step in the direction toward perfection. The actual realization of this comes from the personality of the God-conscious soul as a fragrance in his thought, speech, and action, and proves in the world as incense put on the fire.

There are beliefs such as that of salvation through Christ: and the man who is agitated against religion, closes the doors of his heart before having the patience to understand what really it means. It only means that there is no liberation without an ideal before one. The ideal is a steppingstone towards that attainment which is called liberation.

There are others who cannot conceive the thought of Christ's divinity. The truth is that the soul of man is divine, and that divine spark, when with the unfoldment of the soul it reaches the point of culmination, then deserves being called divine.

And there is a great difference in the beliefs of people who have various opinions about the immaculate birth of Jesus. And the truth is that when the soul arrives at the point of understanding the truth of life in its collective aspect, he realizes that there is only one Father, and that is God; and this world, out of which all the names and forms have been created, is the Mother; and the Son, who is worthy through recognizing the Mother and Father and by serving his Mother and Father, and by fulfilling the aim of creation, is the Son of God.

And then the question of the forgiveness of sin. Is not man the creator of sin? If he creates it, he can destroy it also. If he cannot destroy, his elder brother can. The one who is capable of making, he is capable of destroying. He who can write something with his pen, can rub it with his eraser from the surface of the paper. And when he cannot do it, then that personality has not yet arrived at completeness, at that perfection to which all have to go. There is no end to the faults in man's life, and if they were all recorded, and there was no erasing of them, life would be impossible to live. The impression of sin, in the terminology of metaphysics, may be called an illness, a mental illness. And as the doctor is able to cure illness, so the doctor of the soul is able to heal. And if people have said that through Christ sins are forgiven, that can be understood in this way, that love is that shower by which all is purified. No stain remains. What is God? God is Love. When His mercy, His compassion, His kindness are expressed through a God-realized personality, then the stains of one's faults, mistakes, and wrong-doings are washed away, and the soul becomes as clear as it has always been. For in reality no sin nor virtue can be engraved or impressed upon a soul; it can only cover the soul. The soul in itself is Divine Intelligence; and how can Divine Intelligence be engraved either with sin or virtue, or happiness or unhappiness? For the time it becomes covered with the impression of happiness or unhappiness; and when these clouds are cleared from it, then it is seen to be divine in its essence.

And the question of the crucifixion of Christ, apart from its historical aspect, may be explained in that the life of the wise is on the cross all the time. The wiser the soul will become, the more it will realize the cross. Because it is the lack of wisdom which causes the soul to do all actions, good or bad. As it becomes wise, the first thing is that its action is suspended. And the picture of that suspension of action becomes a picture of helplessness, the hands nailed and the feet nailed; neither can he go forward, nor can he go backward, nor can he act, nor can he move. And this inaction outwardly may show helplessness, but in point of fact is the picture of perfection.

There are two questions which come to the mind.

What is, then, the meaning of the Sacrament, which is said to be symbolical of the Flesh and Blood of Christ? It teaches that those who give importance to the Flesh and Blood of the Master are mistaken; that the true being of the Master was bread and wine. If he had any flesh and blood, it was the bread and wine. And what is bread and wine? The bread is that which is the soul's sustenance; the soul's sustenance is the knowledge of God; it is by this knowledge that the soul lives the eternal life. And the Blood of Christ is the love element, the intoxication of which is a bliss; and if there is any virtue, it all comes from that principle.

And there is another question: that Christ gave his life to save the world. It only explains sacrifice—that no man in this world, going toward the goal, will escape from the test to which life will put him. And that test is sacrifice. At every step towards the final goal, to the Attainment, he will be asked a sacrifice which will be a greater and greater one as he will continue on the path, where he will arrive at a point where there is *nothing*—whether his body or mind, or action or thought or feeling—that he keeps back from sacrifice for others. And it is that by which man proves that realization of divine truth. In short, the Christ-ideal in other words is the picture of the Perfect Man; and the explanation of the Perfect Man and the possibility of the Perfect Man can be seen in the verse of the Bible: "Be ye perfect as your Father in Heaven is Perfect."

The Philosophy of the Sacrament

Man is not only made of flesh, skin, and bone, but he is composed of many fine and gross properties, and therefore, for him to live, many different properties are needed. But generally man considers his food, which nourishes his physical body and seeks for a stimulant for the same body, not knowing that besides this there is much of his being starved all through life for food, and man's ignorance of his other part of being allows that part to be at least dead to his consciousness. The words of Christ, "The spirit quickeneth, the flesh profiteth nothing," are indicative of this.

We trace in the Bible Christ's saying to his followers: "Eat my flesh and drink my blood." What does it mean? It does not mean: "Eat the flesh of my physical body and drink its blood." It means: "The being in which I am living (God's being), have this as the food to nourish your fine being; drink this to stimulate your spiritual being."

There is a verse of Abdal Qader Jilani of Baghdad, "I am the bird of the spiritual spheres dwelling at present in earthly spheres, but my food is the knowledge of God and my drink is His beauty in manifestation." Those who are conscious in the earthly spheres live on earthly food and stimulants; but those who become conscious of the higher world are nourished by the Thought of God, which is their bread; and that which stimulates them as wine is their vision of God in the sublimity of nature, which is the real sacrament, given in churches as a symbol in bread and wine.

Baptism

The custom of baptism has a mystical significance which should be studied from the ideal of the Sufi, and which he calls *Fana*. Sinking the whole body into the water means being as not being, or even living as not living. In other words, it may be said: living, not as the dead are living, but as the really living ones.

The water is symbolical of the ocean, in which there are so many waves and yet it is one ocean. Baptism means sinking in this spiritual ocean, which is the Spirit of God, and in the love of God, in the knowledge of God, and in the realization of God—to become as nothing. From that time to understand that: "I exist no more as myself, as a separate entity; and yet I exist, and this existence is the Existence of God."

This is the main teaching of Sufism; sink into the Consciousness of God, that no trace of one's limited being may be found, at least in one's consciousness. That is, really speaking, the ideal, the path and the goal of all. There is a verse of Ghalib that gives such a beautiful picture of this: "I degraded myself in the eyes of the world by dying. How well had it been, had I been sunk in the water! No one could have seen my funeral; no one would have found my grave!"

The Beatitudes

The essence of all that can teach man to bring out the good that is in his soul is in the Beatitudes as taught by Jesus Christ, the Murshid of Murshids; and, if anybody wants to see it practiced, one may go today and see it in the life that the Sufis live in the East. It is they who have known it properly and have practiced it to their utmost ability. Therefore the real treasure of Christ's teaching is Sufism, though the latter is not called Christianity. However, the name makes no difference so long as the sense is right.

"Blessed are the poor in spirit, for theirs is the Kingdom of Heaven." "Poor in spirit" means mild in ego, and the ego is, as its nature, tyrannical, and all the tyranny there is in the world is only caused by the ego. When the ego is placed before God—in other words, when the ego is illuminated with the knowledge of God— it becomes faded; for it denies its limited being and it realizes the being of God. So it loses all its tyranny and becomes mild, which is being poor in spirit. This makes man's whole life heaven, here and in the hereafter.

"Blessed are they that mourn, for they shall be comforted." All things are given to those who demand, and they only deserve them, and they only can enjoy them. The infant cries when he is hungry and to him the food is given, and it is then that he enjoys it most. So it is with the lovers of God, with the seekers of Truth; when their desire becomes so deep that it makes them mourn, it is then that they are comforted.

"Blessed are the meek, for they shall inherit the earth." There is a saying in Persian, "If your word is sweet, you can win the world." The world is too small when meekness can even win the hearts of men—the heart that can contain a thousand such words.

"Blessed are they which do hunger and thirst after righteousness, for they shall be filled." There are only two paths—the path of light and the path of darkness. The former leads to all joy, while the latter leads to all sorrow. And yet every man does not understand it. The one who understands it, goes after it in its pursuit, for he knows that the only sustenance of his soul is righteousness.

"Blessed are the merciful, for they shall obtain mercy." The warmth in one's feeling draws out the coldness from another person's heart. Therefore one cannot receive mercy either from the earth or from Heaven unless one has himself awakened mercy in his soul.

"Blessed are the pure in heart, for they shall see God." This purity of heart is not only in thought, feeling, and action, but it is the purity which in the Eastern language is called *Safai*, from which word "Sufi" has been said to come—to make the heart pure from all that is besides God. In other words, the heart must see and realize all as God, and God as all.

"Blessed are the peacemakers, for they shall be called the children of God." They only make peace in life who are unbiased, or unselfish, or impartial, and this is the Nature of God, before Whom we all, rich and poor, foolish and wise, are equal; and His mercy is upon all, and He bestows His gifts on all, deserving and undeserving. Therefore those who follow the way of the Heavenly Father are really His deserving sons.

"Blessed are they who are persecuted for righteousness' sake, for theirs is the Kingdom of Heaven." It is easy to be righteous when everything is smooth in life, but when a person is tried, it is difficult to keep to it, for the more righteous you are, the more losses you have to suffer, and, though there may not be a seeming gain by righteousness, still the goal of the righteous is Heaven in the end.

"Blessed are ye when men shall revile you, and persecute you, and say all manner of evil against you falsely, for my sake. Rejoice, and be exceeding glad, for great is your reward in Heaven, for so persecuted they the Prophets which were before you." This is an advice, not only to the followers of Christ, but to the murids, whose Murshid bears a Message, that they can only prove worthy when their faith is so great in the teaching of their teacher that they stand by him and his teaching in all conditions through life, and suffer contentedly all that befalls them from the ignorance of man, as it has been, and will ever be, with everyone, whoever shall give the Message of Truth.

The Meaning of the Symbol of the Cross

The symbol of the cross represents three great secrets. By understanding these secrets one can understand the whole Nature.

The first secret is the secret of form—that every form has been built up on a perpendicular and a horizontal line. Fruit, flower, leaf, in everything one can see the cross as its basis. It becomes fully manifest in the form of man, this being the perfect form. It is perfect because every form of the mineral, vegetable, or animal kingdom has evolved gradually and developed in the human form. One can notice this by studying the indistinct human form even in the mineral and vegetable kingdoms. Not only the animals have a resemblance to man's form and face, but even in the rose you can see man's face indistinctly. In the pebbles by the seashore, in the rocks, in mountains, one sees an indistinct human form. And when one distinguishes the human form in its real aspect, it is nothing but a cross.

There are two spaces, one known to all, and the other known to a mystic. The first space is the one which we see, which we can measure; the other space is that which accommodates within itself this space. For instance, a space of ten, twenty, or even fifty miles can be accommodated—in other words, can be reflected—in the eye, which is hardly one inch wide when measured according to this external space. This shows that the space that the eye has is a different space from the space that it can accommodate within itself. The eye is the representative of the soul. If the eye can accommodate so much space, how much more can the soul accommodate! It can accommodate the whole universe. Therefore this space which we call space in the terms of the mystic is the horizontal space, but that space in which this is reflected is the perpendicular space. It is these two spaces that are termed, in the language of religion, this world and the next world, and it is these two lines that show the sign of the cross.

3. In the beginning, the traveler on the path of morals understands that the whole life is a fight against destruction, a continual destruction that stands before his life. The picture of activity (construction) is the perpendicular line, and the picture of destruction (hindrance) is the horizontal line. But when a person advances from the moral to the spiritual plane, then he sees two paths of attainment, and both necessary at the same time for perfection. One is the expansion of the spirit from a single being to the whole universe, which signifies the horizontal line, and the other is the journey of man to God, from the limited state of being to the Unlimited, which represents the perpendicular line, and in this cross is hidden the secret of perfection.

"Thy Will be Done, in Earth as it is in Heaven"

In the prayer of the Christian Church there is a sentence: "Thy Will be done, in earth as it is in Heaven." This gives a great key to metaphysics. It gives a hint to the seer that His Will, which is easily done in heaven, has difficulty in being done on earth. And who stands against His Will? Man. And where lies the Will of God? In the innermost being of man. And what stands as an obstacle? The surface of the heart of man. And this means struggle in man himself. In him there is the Will of God, as in Heaven, and where there is the obstacle to it, there is the earth.

By this prayer man is prepared to remove the obstacle which stands before the Will of God.

How can we distinguish between these two aspects of will—the Will of God, and the obstacle, which is the will of man? It is easy for a person with a clear mind and open heart to distinguish, if he only knows the secret of it. For to that which is the Will of God, his whole being responds, and in doing His Will his whole being becomes satisfied. When it is his will, only one side of his being is, perhaps, satisfied for a certain time, and there comes a conflict in himself. He himself finds fault with this idea or action; he himself feels dissatisfied with his own being. The wider the scope in which he sees his idea or his action, the more dissatisfied he will become. When in this manner, by the ray of intelligence, one sees life, one begins to distinguish between his will and the Will of God. The kingdom of God, which is heaven, then comes on earth. It does not mean that it disappears from heaven, but it only means that not only heaven remains as a Kingdom of heaven, but even earth becomes a Kingdom of heaven. The purpose behind all this creation is that heaven may be realized on earth; and if one did not realize it on earth, he cannot realize it in heaven.

One may ask: What do I mean by heaven? Heaven is that place where all is the choice of man and everything moves at his command. Heaven is the natural condition of life. When, on earth, life becomes so entangled that it loses its original harmony, Heaven ceases to exist. And the motive of the soul is to gain in life the Kingdom of heaven which it has lost. Nothing does one attain in life which will give that satisfaction which can only be attained by bringing heaven on earth.

Muhammad

Muhammad is the one among the Prophets the account of whose life is to be found in history. Born of the family of Ishmael, Muhammad had in him the prophetic heritage, and, before him, that purpose to be fulfilled, the prophecy of which had been made by Abraham in the Old Testament. The Prophet became an orphan in his childhood, and had known what it is in the world to be without the tender care of the mother and without the protection of the father, when a child. And this experience was the first preparation for the child who was born to sympathize in the pain of others. He showed traces of the sense of responsibility in his boyhood, when looking after his cows. A cowherd came and said: "I will look after your herd, and you may go to the town and enjoy yourself. And then you must take charge of my cows, and I will go there for some time." Young Muhammad said: "No, I will take charge of your herd. You may go, but I will not leave my charge." The same principle he showed through his life.

Some say once, others say twice, others say three times, a miracle happened—that the breast of the Prophet was cut open by the angels, and some say they took something away, and instantly his breast was healed. What was it? It was the poison which is to be found in the sting of the scorpion and the teeth of the serpent; it is the same poison which exists in the heart of man. All manner of prejudice, hatred, bitterness, in the form of envy and jealousy, are the small expressions of this poison, which is hidden in the heart of man. And when this poison is taken away in some form or other, then there is the serpent with its beauty and wisdom, without its poisonous teeth; and so it is with man. Man meets with hardships in life, sometimes too hard to stand for the moment, but often such experiences become as higher initiations in the life of the traveler on the path. The heart of man which is the shrine of God, once purified of that poison, becomes the holy abode where God Himself resides.

As a youth Muhammad traveled with his uncle, who went to Syria on a business trip; and he knew the shortcomings of human nature, which have a large scope to play their role in the world of business; he knew what profit means, what loss means, what both mean in the end. This gave him a wider outlook on life, where he saw how one is eager to profit by the loss of another: that human beings live in this world no better than the large and small fishes in the water, who live upon one another.

When the time came to defend the country against a powerful enemy, young Muhammad stood shoulder to shoulder with the young men of his land to defend his people in their most terrible strife. His sincerity in friendship and honesty in his dealings endeared him to all those far and near, who called him by the name Amin, which means trusty, or trustworthy. His marriage with Khadijah showed him a man of devotion, a man of affection, an honorable man as a husband, as a father, and as a citizen of the town he lived in.

Then came the time of contemplation, that time of the fulfillment of that promise which his soul had brought in the world. There came moments when life began to seem sad, with all the beauty and comfort it could offer. He then sought refuge from that depression in the solitude. Sometimes for hours, sometimes for days, for weeks, sitting in the mountains of Gare Hira, he tried to see if there was anything else to be seen. He tried to hear if there was anything to be heard. He tried to know if there was anything to be known. Patient as Muhammad was, he continued in the path of the search after Truth. In the end he began to hear a word of inner guidance: "Cry on the Sacred Name of Thy Lord"; and as he began to follow that advice, he found the re-echo of the word his heart repeated in all things of Nature; as if the wind repeated the same name as he did; the sky, the earth, the moon, and the planets, all said the same name that he was saying. When once in tune with the Infinite, realizing his soul one within and without, the call came: "Thou art the man; go forward into the world and carry out Our command; glorify the name of God; unite them who are separated; waken those who are asleep, and harmonize one with the other, as in this is the happiness of man."

Often Khadijah found Muhammad had covered himself with a mantle, that he might not see himself, trembling at the sight of the responsibility that was thrown on him. But she kept telling him: "You are the man, a man so kind and true, so sincere and devoted, forgiving and serving. It is your part of work to perform; fear not; you are destined to it by the Almighty; trust in His great power; in the end success will be yours."

The day when Muhammad gave his Message, to his surprise, not only the enemies, but the friends who were near and dear to the Prophet, turned against, would not listen to a new gospel taught. Through the insults and the harm and injury they caused him and those who listened to him, he still continued, in spite of being exiled from home three times; and proved in the end, as every real Prophet must prove, that Truth alone is the conqueror, and to Truth belongs all victory.

The God of Islam

Islam has in every period held the idea of a formless God; but especially in the period when the Prophet Muhammad came— whose Message, since his coming, was named by the same name, *Islam*—great stress was put upon the idea of a formless God. It is difficult for man to make God intelligible if he does not give Him any form; and yet a step higher in the realization of God is to make Him intelligible beyond the limit of form. God, therefore, in Islam, was made intelligible by His attributes. As Creator, as Father, as Mother, as Sustainer, as Judge, as Forgiver, as the Source and the Goal of this whole manifestation, One Who is always with His creature, within him, without him, Who notices all his feelings, thoughts, and actions, Who draws the line of man's fate, before Whom man must appear to give his account, is the God of Islam.

Islam believed in One Only God with many attributes, and yet beyond any attributes; invisible, and beyond the comprehension of man; Almighty; Incomparable; no one save He having any power beside Him; the Knower of all things, and pure from all impurities; free from all things, and yet not far from all things; in Him all abiding, and He living in all. The whole essential teaching of Islam (which is called *Kalamat*) tends to explain clearly the oneness of God; and yet the attributes are suggested, not in order to explain God, but with a view to make God intelligible to the human mind.

These attributes form the external part of God, which is intelligible to man, which is named *Sifat*; but that which is hidden under attributes, and that which cannot be intelligible to the human mind, that part of the Divine Being is the real Being, and that Being is called *Zat*. The whole tendency of Islam has been to disentangle man's heart from such thoughts of God as limit and divide Him, and to clear man's heart from duality, which is the nature of this illusory world, and to bring him to that atonement with God which has been the real aim and intention of every religion.

Forms of Islamic Worship

The form of Islamic worship shows the improvement on the form of worship in the human evolution, for Islam prefers Nature to art: to see in it the Immanence of God when at worship.

The call of the muezzin for prayer before sunrise, and his call when the sun is at its zenith; his call at sunset; the prayers in the afternoon, in the early evening, and at midnight, all suggest to the seer that, while worshiping God, a revelation from Him through the tongue of Nature was sought. It is said in the Qur'an: "Cry in the name of thy Lord, the most beneficent, Who hath by His Nature's skillful pen taught man what he knew not," which means: "Who has written this world as a manuscript by His pen of Nature."

If you desire to read the Holy Book, read it in Nature. There are several *suras* which support this thought. As is said in the Qur'an: "By the night when it covers, by the day when it brightens, by what created the male and female, verily your aims are diverse." Read in the manuscript of Nature that diversity is natural; the very covering and brightening of the light in Nature, and the difference between male and female, show that your aims should be diverse.

The laws of cleanliness are strictly observed in Islam: that no one is to offer prayer without an ablution, which is taught as a preparatory part of his worship.

The worship of Islam embraces in it a universal code of humility—that the customs existing in all parts of the world of bowing and bending and prostrating are all devoted to the One Being only, Who alone deserves it, and no one else. The beauty in this is that, when man—the most egoistic being in creation, who keeps himself veiled from God, the Perfect Self within, by the veil of his imperfect self, which has formed his presumed ego—by the extreme humility when he stands before God and bows and bends and prostrates himself before His Almighty Being, makes the highest point of his presumed being, the head, touch the earth where his feet are, he in time washes off the black stains of his false ego, and the light of perfection gradually manifests. He stands then first face to face with his God, the idealized Deity, and when the ego is absolutely crushed, then God remains within and without, in both planes, and none exists save He.

The Duties of the Faithful in Islam

There are four duties of the faithful as taught in Islam. The number four conveys mystically squareness and balance.

The first is *Salat*, the prayers five times a day, the continual balance between work and rest, and rest especially in God, in Whom is the only rest of every soul. The life in the world is such that it absorbs every moment of man's time, and the innate yearning for peace that every soul has is never satisfied. Therefore the prayer five times a day is not too much, considering how far the life in the world removes a soul from God. In my mind, if it were a hundred times a day it would be too little.

The second is *Zakat*, charity. However pious and godly a person may be, however much time of his life he devoted to piety, he cannot deserve the blessing of God unless he is charitable, for charity is the only test of selflessness. All love and friendship is proved by service and sacrifice, and to the extent one is able to do it, one is selfless. And, self being the only barrier that stands between man and God, charity is the only means to break down that barrier, that man may be face to face with God.

Once someone asked the Prophet: "Who is the most blessed, the prayerful, the fasting, the pilgrim, or the charitable?" The

Prophet answered: "The charitable; for he can pray, and he can build a mosque for others to pray; he can fast, and he can help those who fast by giving them rest and peace, by providing for the families that depend on them for maintenance; he can make pilgrimage, and he can send many on pilgrimage. Therefore all these four blessings are involved in one, the charitable."

The third duty is *Roza*, fasting. Man is so dependent on food that even in his infancy, when he is an angel, a king in himself, he hungers after food. This shows that what man needs most in life is food. He will give his diamonds and gold and all his treasure when the time comes that there is lack of bread. Therefore abstaining from food is as abstaining from the dearest thing in life, and sacrificing all comfort, joy, rest, and happiness. As renunciation of lower things is the only means of attainment of higher objects, there can be no better means to attain spiritual life than fasting. Fasting crushes not only the appetite, but the root of all desire that binds the soul, which is the bird of Paradise, to earth's lower regions. Jesus Christ went to the mountain and fasted for forty days against the temptations of the Devil, whom, at the end of fasting, he conquered.

The fourth duty of the faithful is *Hajj*, pilgrimage. Abraham, the father of the nations, and the fountain from which the streams such as Moses, Christ, and Muhammad came, had made a prayer, as it is said in the Qur'an, when leaving his son Ishmael in the barren desert of Arabia. His heart was broken, and there came out of it a prayer: "O Lord, bless this land, that it may become the attraction of the whole world." And so it happened in the course of time that the Word of God was born among the descendants of Ishmael, Muhammad, who glorified the name of the Lord of Abraham aloud, which was heard from the depths of the earth to the summit of heaven, and re-echoed from the north to the south pole; which shook the nations and stirred up races, and so pierced through the hearts of men that the desert, which bore no fruit, no treasure of any kind—no beauty of scenery, no charm of climate—became a center of attraction for numberless souls, who came from all parts of the world and assembled in that land of bliss, king and pauper standing shoulder to shoulder, both recognizing the equality of men in the Presence of God. The strong and weak, rich and poor, high and low, civilized and uncivilized, all come year by year on pilgrimage to Mecca in this land, clad in one piece of cloth, for all to look alike, and to show to God and humanity the equality of the human brotherhood. This is called *Hajj* in Islam.

The Four Grades of Knowledge in Islam

In Islam there is no caste, as the Message was meant to be for uniting humanity in one brotherhood, and yet it was found necessary to train the individuals according to their evolution in life. A training was given in four classes, namely, *Shariat*, *Tarikat*, *Haqiqat*, and *Marifat*.

Since the world of Islam became busy in national and social affairs, the *Shariat* was held fast by the religious authorities and *Tarikat* only with a few pious ones, who sought the door of a Sufi, wanting an initiation in the inner light which was contained in the two remaining classes, *Haqiqat* and *Marifat*.

The two immediate disciples of the Prophet, Ali and Sadik, were initiated by the Prophet, and were the great Masters of the inner teachings of the knowledge of God. Besides, the Sufis who existing during the time of the Prophet were benefited by the presence of the Prophet and the inspiration they gained in Sufism, to which one soon reaches through the path of *Shariat*, *Tarikat*, *Haqiqat*, and *Marifat*.

Shariat means the law that it is necessary for the collectivity to observe, to harmonize with one's surroundings and with one's self within. Although the religious authorities of Islam have limited it to restrictions, yet a thousand places in the Qur'an and Hadith one can trace where the law of *Shariat* is meant to be subject to change to suit the time and place. The law of *Shariat*, unlike any other religious law, deals with all aspects of life, and it is therefore that the Prophet of Islam had to experience personally all aspects of life. The Prophet as an orphan, as a warrior, as a politician, as a merchant, as a shepherd, as a king, as a husband, as a father, as brother, as son and grandson, had to play different parts in the world's various aspects of life before he was prepared to give this divine law.

Tarikat is the understanding of law besides following it, that we must understand the cause of all things that we must do and must not do, instead of obeying the law without understanding. Those who are not evolved are supposed to have faith and to submit to the law. It is for those whose intelligence does not accept things that cannot answer their reason.

Haqiqat is to know the truth of our being and the inner law of Nature. This knowledge widens the heart of a person. When he has realized the truth of being, he has realized the One Being; he is different from nobody, distant from no one: he is one with all. That is the grade where religion ends and Sufism begins.

Marifat is the actual realization of God, the One Being, when there is no doubt anywhere.

When these four classes are accomplished, then the full play of Sufism comes. Sufi means *Safi*, pure—not only pure from differences and distinctions, but even pure from all that is learnt and known. That is the state of Allah, the pure and perfect One.

The Idea of Halal and Haram in Islam

In Judaism there has existed an idea concerning eating and drinking and everything that is done, that certain things are allowed and certain things forbidden, and the same ideas were perhaps developed a little more in Islam. Those who have followed them have obeyed the law of religion, and those who have understood them have found the truth. Of edible things, flesh in particular, the flesh of certain beasts and birds and of certain creatures living in the water was forbidden. The only reason underlying this law was the protection of man against eating anything that he might like, which may perhaps hinder his spiritual evolution.

As all things that man eats and drinks have their cold and warm effect on man's body, and to a certain extent on man's mind, so, especially with animal food, it is natural that man should partake of the quality of the animal he eats. The pig was particularly pointed out, both by Judaism and Islam, as the forbidden animal. Besides many other reasons, the chief reason was that if one can observe, comparing the life of the pig with that of other animals, it will prove to be the most material, regardless of what it eats, blind in passion, and without the faculty of love and affection. The dog also, and the cat, and all carnivorous animals, were considered, from the hygienic point of view, *Haram*, unwholesome, and the people who have made use of their flesh as food have realized that its effect upon their bodies and minds is harmful.

Then there has been a law among Islamic and Judaic people that the animal that is used for food should be made *Zebah*, which means that it should be killed in a certain way. People believed in this as a religious faith, and did not understand the truth at the back of it, and refused to eat meat coming from people who did not follow their religion. The reason was that people should not eat dead animals or birds, considering their flesh to be as wholesome as that of freshly killed animals. And behind it there is a philosophy—that it is not only flesh that benefits man as a desirable food, but the life that still exists in the flesh is the secret of the vigor and freshness that flesh food gives man; when the life is gone out of it, to eat it is like eating dead flesh; it is flesh, and yet there is no life in it. That is why it was made a religious custom—so that if they did not understand its scientific and philosophical point, they might at least follow it because it is their religion.

Then intoxicating drinks were made *Haram*, especially during the time of the Prophet, who accepted milk, it is said in a tale, from an angel who had brought before him two bowls, one of wine, the other of milk. Milk is considered, even by Vedantists, as a *Sattvic* food, a food that gives rest, comfort, and wisdom, whereas wine is considered as a *Rajasic* food, which gives joy, pleasure, confusion, excitement, and happiness for the time. As its results have shown its weak part in all ages to all peoples, that explains why it was forbidden. But, besides that, the philosophical fact is that all things that are made of decayed substance, whether flesh or herb or fruit, have lost the life from them; and the idea is to touch the life in eating and in drinking and in everything that is done, until one is able to touch the Life Eternal, which alone is the innate yearning of the soul.

Namaz

Namaz—prayer—is an inherent attribute in every soul. Whatever and whoever appears to man beautiful, superior, precious, wins him, and he surrenders himself, conscious of his imperfection and dependence upon the object or being that has conquered him. It is therefore that there have been so many objects, such as the sun, moon, planets, animals, birds, spirits, and men, that different individuals have worshiped—whichever appealed to them, according to their evolution. But the inspired souls have from the first day of creation realized that all the objects and beings which bowed down the head of the admirer are in appearance many, but in existence One. Therefore the One is idealized as the Supreme Being, as the Sovereign of both worlds, as God. While all worshiped many, they only worshiped the One, and have taught, under whatever religion it may have been, the same truth, bowing to that One Who alone deserves all kinds of worship.

As there have been so many kinds of people in the world, so many customs and manners, so one bowed differently from the other. In one country people bent down; in the other country they folded the hands; in one country people knelt down; in the other they prostrated themselves. The *Namaz*, therefore, was a form adopted to reconcile all and combine all customs in one form of worship, that they may not fight on the forms of worship when they all worship One and the Same God.

For the rise of every object or affair, its highest point should touch the utmost depth. The soul, which has descended on earth from its existence in the heavens and which has presumed for the time that it is this material body, rises again to its pristine glory on laying the highest part of the presumed self upon the ground. The mechanism of the body is kept in order by the regular action of the breath through every part of the body and by the regular circulation of the blood in all parts of the body, which can be properly done by the highest part of the body—the head—being placed on the ground.

The world is constituted, in its living beings, of egos, one ego assuming several forms and becoming several egos. Among this variety of egos everyone claims perfection, for it is the nature of the real ego within. Upon examination, this ego proves to be imperfect, for it is the imperfect division of the perfect ego. It is not perfect, yet it claims perfection in its ignorance, and longs for perfection when wise. This perfection the imperfect ego can only attain by practicing in the way of worship and of life in the world, in which he may show such humility, meekness, and gentleness that this false presumption which has formed the imperfect ego may be crushed; then what remains will be the perfect ego. *Namaz* is the first lesson for this attainment.

Idolatry

Idolatry seems to have been prevalent through all ages as a principal form of religion, though the names of the gods have differed among different people. The idea of gods and goddesses came from the two sides of man's nature—one idealism and the other veneration. Man, however primitive in his evolution, had, it seems, a desire to look up to some object or some being, as higher and better than himself. Sometimes he created an ideal from his own nature, and sometimes he was helped to such an ideal by another. There is no race in the world that can say, "We never had idolatry among our race"—although many there are who would today look at it with contempt.

Man has known God more from goodness than from greatness, for no man admires power. Man surrenders to power—that is all that is due to it—but man admires goodness. Therefore there are two things that have brought about the ideal of worship: praise of goodness and surrender to a greater power. Support, protection, providence, mercy, compassion, forgiveness were counted as goodness. The creation and destruction of everything and all things were accounted as power. Combining these two, goodness and greatness, man completed the idea of God, and, since God is one, he could not make Him two; though as many men as there are, so many gods there are, since each person's ideal is peculiar to himself.

Man, who could not complete the ideal without forming an idea of personality, could only be satisfied by some certain form, which he would naturally prefer to make rather like his own, or at least he would make a combination of different likenesses, or any likeness that his mind could grasp. As one man has differed from others in his ideas and thoughts, so each differed from his fellow men in his choice of the ideal idol. Therefore, if one called a particular idol "my god," and his friends and followers and relations also accepted that god, then the one who was opposed to that person said, "My god is different from yours," and he made another god. If any disadvantage came from idol worship, it was only this: that instead of bowing to one God, and uniting with his fellow creatures in the worship of one God, men have taken different and separate routes in the name of different idol-gods, and many idolators turned their backs on one another.

Idol worship has been taught to mankind that man might learn to idealize God even if he were not developed enough to understand the ideal of God in its true sense. This was a training, as a little girl receives her first training in domestic life by playing with dolls. Man can only idealize God as man, for, in the first place, every being sees in another himself. A rogue would be afraid of the roguery of another, and a kind person would be expecting kindness from his fellow man. Man has always thought of ghosts, spirits, jinns, fairies, and angels as being in human form! Although sometimes, to make them different, he has added to them wings or horns or a tail, yet he has kept them as close to the human form as possible. And so it is no wonder that his highest ideal he has pictured in the form of man, and has called it the reverse; instead of saying, "I have created God in my own image," he says, "We have created man in Our own likeness." Even such ideals as the idea of liberty are pictured by the man of today in the form of a woman or man, the sign of which exists in the port of New York and on the postage stamps of France.

Man has in all ages been dramatic. He is an actor by nature, and it is his great pleasure to make his life a drama and play a part in it himself. It is this spirit also that is hidden under the church and nation, and it is this spirit which wears a crown and accepts the patched robes of a dervish. And when this same natural attitude plays its part in religious or spiritual life, its first tendency is to place before itself a Lord, a King, a Master, before whom to bow; and it is this that has given man a tendency to idealize God in a human form or to idealize a human name and form as God.

Though there exists, and there has existed, and there will exist, diversity of religions, faiths, and beliefs, yet human nature will remain always the same everywhere, in all parts of the world and in all ages; and the knower of this nature will understand the religion of all, and all he will consider as belonging to his religion, the only Religion of Wisdom.

Man is accustomed to believe in the reality of things that he can touch and perceive, and any ideal, that is beyond his touch and perception, he believes in and yet cannot be certain of its existence. Not only that, but the absence of that ideal prevents his expression of worship. He doubts and wonders to whom he is praying, whether there exists such a being as God; and, if there exists such a being as God, what He looks like. And, as every person is not capable of a beautiful imagination that could please him, so everyone is not capable of picturing in his mind the ideal of his worship. Therefore it is musicians who have composed music, though everybody can sing or hum a little to amuse himself; and it is the painter who paints a picture, though everybody can draw a little to amuse himself; and so it is the imaginative—those whose imagination reached above the height of the ordinary imagination—who gave a picture of their imagination to the world in the form of a myth which was reproduced by art and made into an idol. This was the only way that in ancient times it seemed best to adopt for the upliftment of humanity.

The Hindus were the first in the world to form the conception of three aspects of the Divinity, which they called *Trimurti*: *Brahma, Vishnu,* and *Shiva* —the Creator, the Sustainer, and the Destroyer. How true it is that these three powers in life seem to keep the balance of the whole universe, and those three aspects work in everything in the world! The picture of *Brahma* was made with four arms, which signifies that, besides the physical arms, there are mental arms, which are necessary in the scheme of creation. And *Vishnu* is pictured seated on the cobra; that means the power of destruction, that is waiting like a cobra to eat every activity—to take away fame from the famous, to take away wealth from the rich, to take away power from the powerful—he who can rest upon that, he is the Sustainer of all activities and interests in life. The picture of *Shiva* is that of an ascetic, from whose head spring rivers, whose neck is a cobra, ashes on his body, a bull his vehicle. In this picture the cobra signifies destruction accepted— all that men fear is wrapped round one's neck; ashes are significant of annihilation—everything that has gone through a perfect destruction turns into ashes; rivers from the head show a constant spring of inspiration, as the inspiration of the mystic is limitless; the bull signifies one with simple faith, who, without reasoning, accepts the truth, which by intellect one can readily accept. There are three goddesses who show the other aspect of these natures: *Saraswathi,* the goddess of *Brahma,* who rides on a peacock, with four hands, two holding a *vina,* in one hand a rosary, in the other a book; which means that music is creative, learning is creative, contemplation is creative, and in art is the beauty which the peacock represents. The goddess of *Vishnu* is *Lakshmi*, who is standing on a lotus, with a crown of gold, with four hands, in one hand a *chakra*, an ancient weapon, in another *kawel*, a lily, which represents that wealth has all the beauty of life at her feet, and delicacy and tenderness in her hands. The weapon represents the power that is needed to hold wealth: two arms, one to collect, the other to give; the crown of gold signifies that the honor of the wealthy is his wealth. These are lessons given to humanity to study the different aspects of life with the thought of sacredness.

The Universe, to the eyes of the wise in all ages, has become one single Immanence of the Divine Being; and that which cannot be compared, or which has no comparison, was difficult to explain in the human tongue. Therefore, the idea of the wise in all ages has been to allow mankind to worship God in whatever aspect they may be capable of picturing Him. One can trace back in histories and traditions that trees were worshiped; animals and birds; rivers and seas; planets, the sun and moon, were worshiped; heroes were worshiped, of all kinds; there has been worship of ancestors, of spirits, both good and evil; and the Lord of Heaven was worshiped by some as the Creator; by some as the Sustainer; by some as the Destroyer; by some as the King of all. And the wise have tolerated all aspects of worship, seeing that they all worship the same God in different forms and names, and yet do not know that another person's god is the same God Whom each has worshiped. Therefore the religion of the Hindus was to see these many gods in one God, and to recognize that one God in all His myriad forms.

There came a time when God was raised from idol to ideal, and it was an improvement, no doubt. And yet even in the ideal He is still an idol, and unless the question of life and its perfection were solved by the ideal of God, by one's love and worship of Him, one has not arrived at the object for which religion stands.

The need of the God-Ideal is like the need of a ship to sail through the Ocean of Eternity; and as there is danger of sinking in the sea without a ship, so there is danger of falling a prey to mortality for the man without the God-Ideal. The difficulty of the believer has always been no less than the difficulty of the unbeliever. For a simple believer, as a rule, knows God from the picture that his priest has given him—God the Good, or Cherisher, or Merciful; and when the believer in the Just God sees injustice in life, and the believer in the Kind God sees cruelty around him, and when the believer in the Cherisher God has to face starvation, then comes the time when the cord of his belief breaks. How many in this late war have begun to doubt and question the existence of God, and some became quite unbelievers.

Idolatry, in a way, has been a lesson to practice one's faith and belief patiently before heedless gods of stone, and to prostrate oneself and bow before the idol god whom man's own hands have made. No answer from him in man's distress, no stretching out the hand in man's poverty, no caress or embrace of sympathy comes from that heedless god; and yet faith and belief is retained under all circumstances, and it is such belief, which is founded on the foundation of rocks, that stands in the rains and storms unshaken and unbroken. And, after all, which is the abode of God? It is man's belief. And upon what is He seated? His throne is man's faith. So idolatry was the primary stage of strengthening faith and belief in God, the ideal which alone is the source of the realization of Truth.

An Advanced Form of Idolatry

When the world evolved to such a stage that a believer in God was able to see even in the idol his God, and communicate with Him by the power of his faith, then came the next lesson for the faithful, which one sees in the series of Prophets coming one after the other to Beni Israel. From Abraham to Moses, from Moses to Christ, the lesson came which culminated in the Message of Muhammad. The idea was to learn the next lesson—of turning the idol into an ideal, rising from the worship of form to the abstract. By prayer, by praising the Lord, by glorifying His name, by contemplating upon His attributes, by admiring His righteousness, and by realizing His goodness, man created his God in his heart. Idolatry was meant for this, but it was the first lesson; the second was to free one's mind from the form; since there are numerous forms, and when God is recognized in one form, then all other forms are left out, not being recognized as His forms also.

Man has in his nature a weakness, and that is that when anything is given to him for his good, and when he likes it, he becomes attached to it until he gets its bad results; and, once he is attached, he never wishes to leave it. If a physician gives a drug to his patient and the patient likes it, he indulges in it, and wishes to continue it, until, instead of a medicine for his cure, it turns into a vice for his destruction. So idolatry became a vice, until the Messengers had to fight it and break it with the hammer. But in cases where it has remained as a first lesson, it has made a great improvement, and has made people much more capable of receiving the second lesson of the God-Ideal, which for many has been difficult to learn.

The Higher Form of Idolatry

No doubt it is true that God cannot be worshiped without idolatry in some form or other, although many people would think it absurd. God is what man makes Him, though His True Being is beyond the capacity of man's making, or even perceiving. Therefore the real belief in God is unintelligible; only that part of God is intelligible which man makes. Man makes it in the form of man, or in the attributes which seem to him good in man; and that is the only way of modeling God, if man ever does so. To make a statue of stone in some form and to worship it as God is the primitive stage of worship; but to picture God in a human form, in the form of some Hero, Prophet, or Savior, is an advanced kind of worship. But when man worships God for His goodness—in other words, impressed by the sublimity of His nature—when man holds the vision of Divine Beauty, recognizing the beauty in merit, power, or virtue; and when he sees this in its perfection, and he calls it God, Whom he worships, then it is a higher kind of worship. This stage of God-realization is a step forward from the realization of the Deity in a limited human form.

This influence was brought in the Hindu religion mostly during the time of Shankara Charya, who did not interfere with the others who were in the primitive stage and worshiped idols, but tried throughout his life, in a very intelligent and gentle way, to make the Truth known wisely in his land, which was spread slowly; yet its influence has been helpful. In the Semitic races this higher form of worship is known to have been introduced by Abraham, and it is this idea which was called Islam, which sometimes disappeared and sometimes appeared during the time of different prophets mentioned in the Bible, and became materialized more during the time of Muhammad, when a nation formed and was made the custodian of a religion, the main spirit of which was this idea; and it was called by the same name as its origin, *Islam*. There cannot be a greater proof of this fact than the name of the holy city, *Dar-as-Salaam* (which is known in the West, in a corrupt form, *Jerusalem*), Gate of *Salaam*, or *Islam*, Peace. This name existed very long before the coming of Muhammad. Therefore the word Islam has its origin in this ideal, although afterwards it became the name of a nation that held this ideal.

The Sufi's Conception of God

The idea of God is a means for the Sufi to rise from imperfection to Perfection, which is suggested in the Bible: "Be ye perfect, as your Father in Heaven is Perfect." There is a vast gulf between the state of imperfection and the state of Perfection, and God is the boat in which one sails from the port of imperfection to Perfection.

To a Sufi, God and man are not two; the Sufi does not consider God separate from himself. The Sufi's God is not in Heaven alone; He is everywhere. He sees God in the unseen and in the seen; he recognizes God both within and without. Therefore there is no name which is not the Name of God, and there is no form which is not the form of God, to the eyes of the Sufi. As Jelal-ud-Din Rumi says: "The Beloved is all in all; the lover only veils Him; the Beloved is all that lives; the lover a dead thing." In other words, he means that this dual aspect of love which is expressed as lover and beloved, is in fact one, and that one will die and one alone will live. The one that will die is the imperfect self which covers Perfection; the One that will live is the Perfect Self.

The Sufi recognizes both these aspects in himself, the imperfect and mortal aspect of his being and the Perfect, the Immortal, Aspect of his Being. The former his outer self represents; the latter is his innermost self. Since the imperfect self covers his soul and confines it in a limited being, he recognizes at the same time the greatness of the Perfect Being, and calls himself "I," a servant of God, and God the Lord of the whole existence. In the Sufi schools in the East this idea is expressed in a Qur'an allegory which moves those who enjoy its poetic delicacy. In the Qur'an it is related that, when the first man was made, he was asked: "Say, who is thy Master?" and he answered, "Thou art my Lord."

Philosophically, this idea is the picture of human life. Man begins his life on earth by accepting somebody's command, fearing lest he cause him any displeasure, looking upon someone as his support, protector, or guide, be it in the form of father or mother, a relation, friend, master, or king, which shows that man begins his life in the world with his imperfection, at the same time recognizing, surrendering, and bowing to perfection in whatever form. When man understands this better, then he knows that all sources that demanded his surrender, or recognition, were limited and powerless in comparison to that perfect ideal which we call God. Therefore, it is the same attribute that the ordinary man has toward another who is greater than he in strength, power, or position, that the Sufi learns to show toward his God, the ideal of Perfection, because in God he includes all forms in which he recognizes beauty, power, greatness, and perfection. Therefore the worship of the Sufi is not alone worship of the Deity; by worship he means to draw closer to perfection; by worship he tries to forget his imperfect self in the contemplation of the Perfect One.

It is not necessary that the Sufi should offer his prayers to God for help in worldly things, or by thanking Him for what he receives, although this attitude develops in man a virtue that is necessary in life. By the thought of God, the whole idea of the Sufi is to cover his imperfect self even from his own eyes, and that moment when God is before him, and not his own self, is the moment of perfect bliss to him. My Murshid, Abu Hashim Madani, once said that there is only one virtue and one sin for a soul on this path: virtue when he is conscious of God and sin when he is not. No explanation can be sufficient to describe the truth of this except the experience of the contemplative, to whom, when he is conscious of God, it is as if a window is open which is facing Heaven, and, when conscious of the self, the experience is the opposite. For all the tragedy of life is caused by consciousness of self. Every pain and depression is caused by this, and anything that can take away the thought of the self helps to a certain extent to relieve man from pain; but God-consciousness gives a perfect relief.

The Symbology of
Religious Ideas

Symbology

The wise have given lessons to the world in different forms suited to the evolution of the people at a particular time, and the first and most original form of education that the wise gave to the world was symbolical. This method of teaching has been valued in all ages, and will always have its importance. That is not beauty which is not veiled. In the veiling and unveiling of beauty is the purpose of life. Beauty is that which is always out of reach. You see it and you do not see it. You touch it and you cannot touch it. It is seen and yet veiled; it is known and yet unknown. And therefore words are often inadequate to express the beauty of Truth. Therefore symbolism is adopted by the wise.

The religions of the old Egyptians, of the ancient Greeks, of the Hindus, and of the Parsis, all have symbols which express the essential Truth hidden under a religion. There is a symbolism in Christianity, and in many ancient religions of the world. Man has often rebelled against symbolism; but it is natural: man has always revolted against things he cannot understand. There has been a wave of opposition to symbolism in both parts of the world, the East and the West. It came in the East in the period of Islam, and in the West it re-echoed in the Reformation. No doubt when the sacred symbols are made as patents by the religious who want to monopolize the whole Truth for themselves, then it gives rise to that tendency of human nature which is always ready to accept things or reject them. However, one can say without exaggeration that symbology has always served to keep the ancient wisdom intact for ages. It is symbology that can prove today the saying of Solomon: "There is nothing new under the sun." There are many thoughts relating to human nature, the nature of life, relating to God and His many attributes, and relating to the path towards the goal, that are expressed in symbolism.

To a person who sees only the surface of life, symbols mean nothing. The secret of symbols is revealed to souls who see through life, whose glance penetrates through objects. Verily, before the seer the things of the world open themselves. And it is in this uncovering of things that beauty is hidden. There is a great joy in understanding, especially in understanding things that to most people mean nothing. It requires intuition, even something deeper than intuition—insight—to read symbols. To the one to whom symbols speak of their nature and of their secret, each symbol is in itself a living manuscript. Symbology is the best means of learning the mysteries of life, and one of the best ways of leaving behind ideas which will keep for ages after the Teacher has passed away. It is speaking without speaking; it is writing without writing. The symbol may be said to be an ocean in a drop.

The Symbol of the Sun

Light has the greatest attraction for the human soul. Man loves it in the fire and in things that are bright and shining, and that is why he considers gold and jewels as precious. The Cosmos has a greater attraction for him than the earth, because of the light. As man evolves, he naturally ceases to look down on earth, but looks up to the Cosmos, the Heavens. The most attractive object that he sees is the sun in the heavens, the sun which is without any support and is more luminous than anything else in the heavens. Therefore, as man is attracted to beauty and surrenders to beauty, he bows to the sun as being the greatest beauty in heaven, and man took the sun as Nature's symbol of God.

This symbol he pictures in different forms. In Persia, China, Japan, India, Egypt, whenever God was pictured, it was in the form of the sun. In all ages man has pictured his Prophet, Master, Savior, with a sun around his head. In ancient Persia there used to be a golden disc behind the head of the king, picturing him as the sun, and they used to call this disc *Zardash*. The name Zarathustra has the same origin; the word simply meant the golden disc. In Hindu temples and Buddhist temples around the image of different Avataras there is this sign of the sun, and this symbol was used both in the East and in the West in turbans and hats. There are now people in India who put on their turbans a brass band, which represents the sun.

A deeper study of the sun suggests the four directions of lines that are formed around it. It is this sign that is the origin of the symbol of the cross. The ancient traditions prove that the idea of the cross existed in the East long before the coming of Christ, especially among the Brahmans. It is from this sign that the two sacred arms were made, *Chakra* and *Trissoun*. Islam, the religion which allows no symbolism, has in the building of the mosques the same symbolism of the sun. Whether the name of the sun be written in Persian or in Arabic, it makes the form of the mosque.

Man, as happens to be his nature, has blamed the sun

worshipers and mocked at them, but he has never been able to uproot the charm, the attraction for human souls held by the sun.

The Brahman Symbolical Form of Worship

Puja is the name of the Brahman form of worship, which is, from the beginning to the end, a symbolical expression of what the seeker has to perform on the path of spiritual attainment. After bathing in the running stream of water, which the Hindu calls the Ganges (whatever be the name of the river, he at that time believes that it is the Ganges, the sacred river), he proceeds with flowers to the shrine of the deity. He puts onto the deity the flowers, and repeats the mantram, and stands greeting the deity with folded hands, and prostrates himself before the deity. Then he rings the bell and repeats the sacred word. Then he takes rice in his hands and puts it at the feet of the deity. Then the red powder, *coucou*, he touches with the tip of his finger; and makes a mark with it on the shrine of the deity and then on his own forehead. Then he touches the ointment with the tip of his finger, and, after touching the deity, he touches his forehead with the same ointment. He then prostrates himself, and makes three circles around the shrine. Then he rings the bell, and thus the service is finished. Afterwards he goes and stands before the sun, and does his breathing exercises while arising to the sun, and that completes the next part of his worship.

However primitive this form of worship, at the back of it there seems to be a great meaning. The meaning of the bath in the Ganges is to become purified before one makes any effort of journeying on the spiritual path. The purification of the body and of the mind both is necessary before one takes the first step towards the God-Ideal. One must not approach the deity before such purification—the outer purification as well as the inner purification—for then alone, when once a person is pure, he will find it easy to attain the desired Presence. The meaning of the flowers, which he takes, is that God is pleased with the offerings which are delicate, beautiful, and fragrant. Delicacy means tenderness of heart, beautiful in color is fineness of character; fragrance is the virtue of the soul. This is the offering with which God is pleased. He stands with the thought that his self is devoted in perfect discipline to the Supreme Will of God. His hands folded express no action on the part of himself, but complete surrender. The meaning of prostration is self-denial in the right sense of the word, which means: "I am not; Thou art." Whispering the words and ringing the bell is that the same word is rung in the bell of one's heart. His touching the red powder means touching the eternal life; and when he touches the deity with the powder, it means that from this source he is to gain eternal life; when he touches his forehead with it, it means he has gained it for himself. And the ointment means wisdom, and the touching of the god with it and then his forehead means that true Wisdom can be obtained from God alone, and touching his own head with it means that he has gained it. Then making three circles around the shrine is the sign that life is a journey, and that the journey is made to attain his goal, which is God; "Every step I take in my life," the Brahman thinks, "will be in His direction, in the search of God." In the second part of the service, when he stands before the sun, by that he means that God is to be sought in the light. And by the breathing exercises he welds that link of inner communication between God and himself.

The Flute of Krishna

Krishna is pictured in Hindu symbology with a crown of peacock's feathers, playing the flute. Krishna is the idea of Divine Love, the God of Love. And the Divine Love expresses itself by entering into man and filling his whole being. Therefore the flute is the human heart, and a heart which is made hollow will become a flute for the God of Love to play upon. When the heart is not empty—in other words, when there is no scope in the heart—there is no place for love. Rumi, the great poet of Persia, explains the idea more clearly. He says the pains and sorrows the soul experiences through life are as holes made in a reed flute, and it is by making these holes that a player makes out of a reed a flute. Which means, the heart of man is first a reed, and the sufferings and pains it goes through make it a flute, which can then be used by God as the instrument to produce the music that He constantly wishes to produce. But every reed is not a flute, and so every heart is not His instrument. As the reed needs to be made into a flute, so the human heart can be turned into an instrument, and can be offered to the God of Love. It is the human heart which becomes the harp of the angels; it is the human heart which is known as the lute of Orpheus. It is on the model of the heart of man that the first instrument of music was made, and no earthly instrument can produce that music which the heart produces, raising the mortal soul to immortality.

The crown of peacock's feathers leads to a further revelation, that it is the music of the heart which can be expressed through the head; it is the knowledge of the head and the love of the heart that expresses the Divine Message fully. The peacock's feather has in all ages been considered as a sign of beauty and as a sign of knowledge: beauty because it is beautiful, knowledge because it is in the form of an eye. It is by keen observation that man acquires knowledge. Knowledge without love is lifeless. So, with the flute, the crown of peacock's feathers makes the symbol complete.

Water

In the old Scriptures, such as the Vedanta and the Old Testament, spirit is symbolized as water. One wonders why something which is next to earth should be considered as spirit. The nature of water is to give life to the earth, and so the nature of the soul is to give life to the body. Without water the earth is dead; so is the body without soul. Water and earth both mix together; so the spirit mixes with matter and revivifies it. And yet the spirit stands above matter, as water in time lets the earth go to the depth, and stands itself above the earth. But one may ask: "Is the spirit hidden under matter, as the soul in the body?" The answer is: "So does water stay beneath the earth." There is no place where water does not exist; there are places where earth is not to be found; so nowhere in space spirit is absent; only the absence of matter is possible.

The symbolical way of expressing high ideas does not come from the brain; it is an outcome of intuition. The beginning of intuition is to understand the symbolical meaning of different things, and the next step is to express things symbolically. It is in itself a Divine Art, and the best proof of it is to be found in the symbol of water, which is so fitting to express the meaning of spirit.

Wine

Wine is considered sacred, not only in the Christian faith, but in many other religions also. In the ancient religion of the Zoroastrians, *Jami Jamsshyd*, the bowl of wine from which "Jamsshyd drank deep," is a historical fact. Among the Hindus, Shiva considered wine sacred. And in Islam, though wine is forbidden on earth, yet in Heaven it is allowed. Haussi Kaussar, the sacred fountain of Heaven, about which there is so much spoken in Islam, is a fountain of wine.

Wine is symbolical of the soul's evolution. Wine comes from the annihilation of grapes; immortality comes from the annihilation of self. The bowl of poison which is known in many mystical cults also suggests the idea of wine—not a sweet wine, but a bitter wine. When the self turns into something different from what it was before, it is like the soul being born again. This is seen in the grape turning into wine. The grape, by turning into wine, lives; as a grape it would have vanished in time. Only, by turning into wine, the grape loses its individuality, and yet not its life. The selfsame grape lives as wine; and the longer it lives, the better the wine becomes. For a Sufi, therefore, the true sacrament is the turning of one's grape-like personality, which has a limited time to live, into wine; that nothing of one's self may be lost, but, on the contrary, it may be amplified, even perfected. This is the essence of all philosophy and the secret of mysticism.

The Story of Lot's Wife

The ancient method of giving the mystery of life was to give it in the form of a legend. The legend of Lot's wife is that it was to Abraham that Lot was related, and it was by the love and help of Abraham that the two angels were sent to Lot, to warn him of the coming destruction of two cities and to advise him to go to the mountains. And Lot was not willing to leave the cities, but in the end he agreed to. His sons-in-law failed him by not accompanying him, but his wife and his two daughters accompanied him on the journey to the mountains. And they were told that his wife must not look back; and when she did, she was turned into a pillar of salt. Lot and his two daughters remained, and they reached the cave of the mountain, which was Lot's destination.

The two towns that were to be destroyed represent the North Pole and the South Pole, the two poles of the world. For all the treasure of the earth, all possessions and power and fame that belong to the earth, are subject to destruction. And that was taught to Lot, the human soul, who was the relation of Abraham, the divine soul, which is from Brahma, the Creator. The relationship of

Lot with Abraham represents the relation of the human soul to the Creator. The two angels were the angels of light and of reason. When the light comes to man, its first teaching is to warn the soul of the disaster that awaits all that is subject to death and destruction. It is this lesson that is called in Sanskrit the lesson of *Vairagya* —when man's eyes open to see that all that he loves and likes and wishes to hold and possess is subject to destruction and death.

There are five bodies considered by the Mystics of old to be the vehicles of the soul, which are called: *Anandamayakosh*, body of joy; *Vignanamayakosh*, body of wisdom; *Manamayakosh*, body of mind; *Pranamayakosh*, body of ether; *Annamayakosh*, body of earth. This last is the receptacle of food. It lives on earthly food, and if it is starved of that, it dies. For it is made of earth; it lives on earth. The other is the receptacle of ether, which is called *Pranamayakosh*. That part of man's being lives by breath and by taking in the air, and if it is starved of air, it cannot live. These two bodies form the material part, the physical part, of man's being. And it is these two receptacles which are referred to in the legend as the two sons-in-law.

Then there is *Manamayakosh*, which is mind, and the mental body. And this body has its action and reaction on both sides; it acts and reacts on the earthly bodies, and it acts and reacts upon the soul. Therefore when Lot left the two cities, which represent the physical plane, to journey toward the goal of Immortality, his wife was still with him. For it is not necessary for the mental body to stay behind when the journey towards illumination is begun. It is capable of going with the soul towards Eternity. And yet its attachment to earth and the physical plane is great, because it is made, it is built, of physical impressions, of all impressions that come from the physical, world; and of necessity it wants to turn to see if the physical being or the spiritual being is leading it aright. The principal nature of mind is doubt—whether one is doing right or wrong. And doubt and faith are enemies. While faith leads to the destination, doubt pulls back. When the mind was so pulled back, attracted by all the impressions of earthly life, it could neither take hold of the earth nor journey with the spirit, and remained neither earth nor water, but salt.

The only two bodies which are close to the soul followed the soul. Naturally they would follow, for they are closely related to the soul, *Vignanamayakosh*, the body of wisdom, and *Anandamayakosh*, the body of joy. The soul bound towards the Eternal Goal—as it is called, the top of the mountains—then proceeded towards the mountains. And before they reached the top of the mountains, there was the cave, which is called Heaven—in metaphysics, *capacity*; in Sanskrit, *Akasha* —which has the power of holding the soul from going to the top and using the soul for some purpose. And the soul which was bound for the Eternal Goal remained, intoxicated by the ecstasy that it received from the plane of joy and the plane of wisdom. And as everything that happens has its purpose, so this joy resulted in a great purpose, in the birth of the Messenger, which in Sanskrit is called *Bodhisattva*. The Messenger was born of the souls' experience, the knowledge and the happiness, to bring good tidings to the world.

A question may arise, why *Manamayakosh* must be the mother, and *Anandamayakosh* and *Vignanamayakosh* must be the daughters. And the answer is that they are born of mind, born of mind and soul. If there were only the soul, there would be neither joy nor wisdom. Mind and soul both produce joy and wisdom. Therefore the latter are the daughters, because mind is the mother. The two lower planes are represented by the sons-in-law, because they were not directly born of mind and soul; it was a separate substance mind and soul have taken into their life.

By this story the process is taught how the soul can journey from mortality to immortality, and what experiences the soul possibly has to have on its way. But when the Messenger is so created, then the Father—the Soul—rests in peace. It is therefore that the Messenger was called the *Son*, and the Original Soul the *Father*.

Jacob Wrestling with the Angel

The wrestling of Jacob was the wrestling of the soul with the ego. That awakened soul looks about and asks: "Who is my enemy?" And while the ignorant soul thinks: "It is my neighbor, my relation, who is my enemy," the awakened soul says: "It is myself; my ignorant ego is my enemy; and it is the struggle with this enemy that will bring me light and raise me from the denseness of the earth." Night is, symbolically, the time when the darkness of ignorance causes confusion; one feels sorrow, loneliness, depression; one sees no way out; one is burdened on all sides, chained; there seems no freedom for the soul; for this is the time of night. But when the soul can fight the ego, then it rises above the chains and attachments of this world. As it is said in the Bible, first Jacob left all his belongings; he came away from them. This means that he was indifferent to all to which he once felt attached. The Sufi looks at this from another point of view. He thinks that to leave all he possesses, and to go to the forests or mountains, is not true detachment; the true detachment is in the heart of man. One can be surrounded by beauty, comfort, wealth, position, love—all these things—and yet be detached from them; be no slave to them; rise above them.

Jacob left all and came to the solitude, into the silence; and there he wished to fight the deluded self, the ego, which blinds man to the Truth. And what was the result? The daybreak came, and that man, or angel, who had fought with Jacob, wished to depart. This means that the ego wanted to leave; there was no more ego, no more *I*; but with the daybreak a new light, a new inspiration, a new revelation, came. The very ego which Jacob saw as his greatest enemy, in the daylight he recognized as God Himself. The One with Whom all night he had fought, he bowed before Him, he asked His blessing; he asked His Name, for he saw then: "No longer I, but Thou." And the name could not be told, for that was the unveiling of the Unity of God and man, and in this realization names and forms are lost.

Jesus Walking on the Water

The phenomenon of Christ's walking on the water, from a mystical point of view is suggestive of a much greater philosophy than only a phenomenon. The whole universe in all its forms is one single vision of a constant activity. From beginning to end every aspect of life represents motion, and it is the perpetual motion of the whole universe which is called life. Therefore the universe is, so to speak, an ocean of vibrations, and every movement represents a wave. Therefore, the wise have called it, in Sanskrit, *Bhava Sagara*, the ocean of life, and the great devotees have constantly prayed to be liberated, that they may not sink, in this ocean, but that they may be able to swim in it—which is called *Tarana*. And it is the Master Spirit that can rise above these waves of the enormous ocean of life, in which generally the souls are drowned. To be in it, and to be able to stand above it, and to walk on it, is the phenomenon of Christ's walking upon it.

Christ said to the fishermen: "I will make you fishers of men." That meant: "As you spread the net and the fishes come into it, so by spirituality your personality will spread in the atmosphere, and the hearts of men hungering for love will be attracted to you as fishes." The love of Christ for the lamb symbolically expresses that to the Master that soul made a greater appeal which was simple and harmless as a lamb. And the crown of thorns represents tolerance of the thorn-like personalities of which there are so many in the world, constantly pricking with their thorns, consciously or unconsciously; and it is this which makes the sensitive annoyed with life in the world. But the Messenger, whose heart represents the Divine Mother and Father both, cannot but be tolerant, and can take willingly all the thorns that would come to him; for that is his crown, the sign of his Sovereignty in the Kingdom of soul.

Christ said to Peter: "Thou wilt deny me three times before the cock crows." It explains human nature. The faith of man is generally dependent upon the faith of the multitude; if the multitude calls the pebble a diamond, everyone will begin to consider it so and to say so. And if the multitude thought that the diamond was a pebble, then everyone would follow the belief of the multitude. The soul of the Messenger, that comes from above (which the dove represents), which is not made by the world nor known by the world, remains unrecognized till the cock crows and the sun rises. Then his words shine and spread the light to the world; and the souls privileged with some little recognition, but with a great deal of doubt, may believe for a moment, impressed by the power and grace of the Master's personality, and yet may deny a thousand times, and doubt and suspect, being impressed by the influence of the multitude. How true it is, the saying in Hindustani that, "Generally a soul follows the multitude." There are rare souls who believe in their conviction, and remain steady even if it were that the whole world was against their own inner conviction. Verily to the faithful belongs every blessing.

The Symbol of the Cross

The symbol of the cross has many significations. It is said in the Bible: first was the word, and then came light, and then the world was created. And as the light is expressed in the form of the cross, so every form shows in it the original sign. Every artist knows the value of the vertical line and the horizontal line, which are the skeleton of every form. This proves the teaching of the Qur'an, in which it is said that God created the world from His own light. The cross is the figure that fits to every form everywhere.

Morally the cross signifies pain or torture. That means that in every activity of life, which may be pictured as a perpendicular line, there come hindrances, which the horizontal line represents. This shows the nature of life, and that, as it is said, man proposes and God disposes. Somebody asked the great Master, Ali, what made him believe in God, Who is beyond human comprehension. Ali said: "I believe in God because I see that when I alone wish, things are not accomplished." According to the metaphysical point of view, this shows the picture of limitation in life.

The symbol of the cross in its connection with the life of Christ not only relates to the crucifixion of the Master, but signifies the crucifixion that one has to meet with by possessing the Truth. The idea of this Hindu philosophy is that the life in the world is an illusion, and therefore every experience in the life and knowledge of this life is also illusion. The Sanskrit word for this illusion is *Maya*; it is also called *Mithea*, from which the word *myth* comes. When the soul begins to see the Truth, it is, so to say, born again; and to this soul all that appears truth to an average person appears false, and what seems truth to this soul is nothing to that average person; all that seems to that average person important and precious in life has no value nor importance for this soul, and what seems to this soul important and valuable has no importance nor value for the average person.

Therefore he naturally finds himself alone in a crowd which lives in a world quite different from that in which he lives. Imagine living in a world where nobody uses your language. Yet he can live in the world, for he knows its language. And yet to him the life in the world is as unprofitable as to a grown-up person the world of children playing with their toys. A human being who has realized the Truth is subject to all pains and torture in the same way as all other persons, except that he is capable of bearing them better than the others. But, at the same time, while in the crowd everyone hits the other and also receives blows, the knower of Truth has to stand alone and receive them only; this is in itself a great torture. The life in the world is difficult for every person, rich or poor, strong or weak, but for the knower of Truth it is still more difficult, and that in itself is a cross. Therefore for a spiritual Messenger the cross is a natural emblem, to explain his moral condition. But there is a still higher significance of the cross which is understood by the mystic. The significance is what is called self-denial; in order to teach this moral gentleness, humility and modesty are taught as a first lesson. Self-denial is an effect of which self-effacement is the cause. It is that a man says: "I am not; Thou art." For instance, an artist, looking at his picture, says: "It is Thy work, not mine," or a musician, hearing his composition, says: "It is Thy creation; I do not exist." Then that soul is in a way crucified, and through that crucifixion resurrection comes. There is not the slightest doubt that when man has had enough pain in his life, he rises to this great consciousness. But it is not necessary that only pain should be the means. It is the readiness on the part of man to deny his part of consciousness and to efface his own personality which lifts the veil that hides the Spirit of God from the view of man.

The Symbol of the Dove

The bird represents the wayfarer of the sky, and at the same time it represents a being who belongs to the earth and is capable of dwelling in the skies. The former explanation of the bird represents the idea of a soul whose dwelling place is Heaven, and the latter represents the dweller on earth being able to move about in the higher spheres, and both these explanations give the idea that the spiritual man, dwelling on the earth, is from Heaven; they explain also that the spiritual man is the inhabitant of the Heavens and is dwelling on earth for a while.

The pigeon was used as a messenger, to carry a message from one place to another, and therefore the symbol of the dove is a natural one to represent the Messenger from above. Spiritual bliss is such an experience that if a bird or an animal were to have it, it would never return to its own kind. But it is a credit due to man that, after touching that point of great happiness and bliss, he comes into the world of sorrows and disappointments and delivers his Message. This quality can be seen in the pigeon also; when the pigeon is sent, it goes, but it faithfully comes back to the master who sent it. The spiritual man performs this duty doubly: he reaches higher than the human plane, touches the divine plane, and brings the Message from the divine to the human plane. In this way, instead of remaining on the divine plane, he arrives among his fellow men, for their welfare, which is no small sacrifice. But then again he performs a duty to God, from Whom he brings his Message, that he delivers to the human beings. He lives as a human being, subject to love, hate, praise, and blame; he passes his life in the world of attachment and the life that binds with a thousand ties from all sides. Yet he does not forget the place from whence he has come, and he constantly and eagerly looks forward to reach the place for which he is bound. Therefore in both these journeys, from earth to Heaven and from Heaven to earth, the idea of the dove proves to be more appropriate than any other idea in the world.

The Ten Virgins

There is a story in the Bible about ten virgins—the five wise virgins and the five foolish. It was said that the bridegroom was to come, and they were to light their lamps; and five were in time, and brought the oil, and lighted their lamps; and the other five waited until the bridegroom came, and when the bridegroom came, then they went to the five who had lighted their lamps and asked of them oil, and were refused. This story is a symbolic expression of receiving the Message of God. By virgin is meant the soul which is awaiting illumination, innocent and responsive to the light; and by five is meant the multitude. And there are two classes of people; one class is those who have prepared themselves and made ready to receive the Message of God, which is pictured as the bridegroom; and the five foolish are that class in mankind who wait and wait until the Message has come and gone. In all ages there have been these two kinds of souls—one kind who are called in the Scriptures believers, the others who are known as unbelievers.

In every age the prophecy has been made by the Messenger of the time as to the next advent. Sometimes it is said: "I will come," and sometimes: "He will come." "I will come" has been told to those who would recognize the same Spirit of Guidance in every coming of the Messenger; "He will come" has been told to those to whom name and form make a difference, and who cannot recognize the same Spirit in another name and another form. For example, the coming of Jesus Christ was the coming of that Spirit which was expressed in this parable as the bridegroom, and how few at that time recognized Him, and how few received illumination! Only those whose lamps were ready to be lighted. Oil in this parable is love, and the light is wisdom. And when their lamps were lighted, then so many came afterwards; but that blessing and privilege which had come with the Personality of the Master had then gone.

They had to take the benefit of the light that came from the lamps of those whose lamps were lighted, but the chance of lighting their own lamps was lost.

The same is with all things in life. Every moment in our lives is an opportunity which brings a benefit and blessing. And the one who knows how to be benefited by it, and how to be blessed by it, receives the benefit and the blessing. Everyone seems living and awake, but few souls really are living and awake. There are opportunities of benefit and blessing on every plane of one's life—on the physical plane, on the mental plane, on the spiritual plane—and every opportunity is invaluable. But often one realizes the truth when it is too late. There is no greater and better opportunity than the moment that can give a spiritual illumination, a moment when one can receive the blessing of God. It is a priceless moment. Who knows it and understands it and tries to be benefited by it is blessed.

Tongues of Flame

The symbolic meaning of the legend is that there is a period when the soul of the earnest seeker is seeking, when it has not yet found the object it is seeking after. In the lifetime of Jesus Christ, the beauty of the Master's wonderful Personality and the great intoxication of his Presence, and the constant outpouring of the Message that he had to give, was so much for his disciples that it soared beyond what may be called a joy or a happiness, or something which is explainable; and all the blessing that they received and experienced during his Presence was covered by the Master's personality. And the time of realization of that which they had constantly gained came in their lives after that great change when the external Person of the Master ascended, and the capacity of realization became open.

But, after the fifty days following the Crucifixion, when they had had sufficient time to recover from the feeling that had over-taken their hearts, the seeming separation from their beloved Lord prepared them, so to speak, in time, and opened the door of their heart, giving that capacity for receiving the illumination which was constantly pouring out from the Spirit of Guidance, the Alpha and Omega, Who always was and is and will be.

The symbolic interpretation of the tongues of flame rising from the foreheads of the disciples is the light of the Message, the rays of the Christ Spirit in the form of thoughts which were expressed in words. There is a stage in the life of a Seer when the tongue of flame becomes, not only an interpretation of the mystery, but as a reality, as his own experience. The head is the center of knowledge, and, when this organ opens, the light which was covered becomes manifest, not only in idea, but even in form.

And the phenomenon which was shown the next day, when the apostles spoke all different languages, can be rightly interpreted in this sense—that every soul hears its own language. For every soul has its own word, as every soul has its peculiar evolution. And it is therefore that one person cannot understand another person in this world, and it becomes more than a miracle when one finds perhaps one person in the world who can understand one fully, which means that in this world the language of each one is not under-stood by another; and if someone understands a little, one feels at-one-ment with him. It was the illumination of the Christ Spirit which brought exaltation in the lives of the disciples, so that they began to respond to every soul they met, and they became at one with every soul, inspired by the sympathy and love of Christ. And they understood the souls as they saw them, and could speak with souls whose language had never before been understood. Plainly speaking, they heard the cry of every soul, and they answered every soul's cry. The Message means the answer to the cry of every soul. Every great Prophet or Teacher had in his life many followers, attracted to his personality, to his words, to his kindness and love; but those who became as the instrument of his Message, whose hearts became as a flute for the Master to play his music, have always been some chosen few, as the twelve apostles of Christ.

Shaqq-i Sadr: *the Opening of the Breast of the Prophet*

There is a story told in Arabia that the angels descended from Heaven to earth and cut open the breast of the Prophet; they took away something that was to be removed from there, and then the breast was made as before. It is a symbolical expression, which gives to a Sufi a key to the secret of human life. What closes the doors of the heart is fear, confusion, depression, spite, discouragement, disappointment, and a troubled conscience; and when that is cleared away, the doors of the heart open. The opening of the breast, really speaking, is the opening of the heart. The sensation of joy is felt in the center of the breast, also the heaviness caused by depression. Therefore as long as the breast remains choked with anything, the heart remains closed. When the breast is cleared from it, the heart is open. It is the open heart which takes the reflection of all impressions coming from outside. It is the open heart which can receive reflections from the Divine Spirit within. It is the openness of heart, again, which gives power and beauty to express oneself; and if it is closed, a man, however learned, cannot express his learning to others.

This symbolical legend explains also what is necessary in the life of man to allow the plant of divine love to grow in his heart. It is to remove that element which gives the bitter feeling. Just as there is a poison in the sting of the scorpion, and as there is a poison in the teeth of the snake, so there is poison in the heart of man, which is made to be the shrine of God. But God cannot arise in the shrine which is as dead by its own poison; it must be purified first, and made real, for God to arise. The soul who had to sympathize with the whole world was thus prepared, that the drop of that poison which always produces contempt, resentment, and ill feeling against another, was destroyed first. So many talk about the purification of heart, and so few really know what it is. Some say to be pure means to be free from all evil thought of bitterness against another. No one with sense and understanding would like to keep a drop of poison in his body, and how ignorant it is on the part of man when he keeps and cherishes a bitter thought against another in his heart. If a drop of poison can cause the death of the body, it is equal to a thousand deaths when the heart retains the smallest thought of bitterness. In this legend the cutting open of the breast is the cutting open of the ego, which is as a shell over the heart. And the taking away of that element is that every kind of thought or feeling against anyone in the world has been taken away, and the breast, which means the heart, is filled with love alone, which is the real life of God.

Miraj: *the Dream of the Prophet*

A story exists in Islam about the dream of the Prophet, a dream which was as an Initiation in the higher spheres. Many take it literally and discuss it, and afterwards go out by the same door by which they came in. It is by the point of view of a Mystic that one can find out the mystery.

It is said that the Prophet was taken from Jerusalem to the Temple of Peace, which means from the outer Temple of Peace to the inner Temple of Peace. A *Buraq* was brought for the Prophet to ride upon. The angel Jibril accompanied the Prophet on the journey, and guided on the path. *Buraq* is said to be an animal of Heaven which has wings, the body of the horse, and the face of a human being. It means the body connected with the mind. The wings represent the mind, and the body of the *Buraq* represents the human body; the head represents perfection. Also this is the picture of the breath. Breath is the *Buraq* which reaches from the outer world to the inner world in a moment's time. Jibril in this story represents reason.

It is said that the Prophet saw on his way Adam, who smiled looking to one side, and shed tears looking to the other side. This shows that the human soul, when it develops in itself real human sentiment, rejoices at the progress of humanity and sorrows over the degeneration of humanity. The *Buraq* could not go beyond a certain point, which means that breath takes one a certain distance in the mystical realization, but there comes a stage when the breath cannot accompany one. When they arrived near the destination, Jibril also retired, which means that reason cannot go any farther than its limit. Then the Prophet arrived near that curtain which stands between the human and the Divine, and called aloud the Name of God, saying: "None exists save Thou," and the answer came: "True, true." That was the final Initiation from which dated the blossoming of Muhammad's prophetic Message.

Index

About Hazrat Inayat Khan

Hazrat Inayat Khan was born in Baroda, India in 1882 into a family of master musicians. A lineage holder in the four major streams of Indian Sufism, he was sent to the West by his teacher Abu Hashim Madani Chishti "to harmonize East and West" with his music. Inayat Khan left India in 1910 and for 16 years he lived and taught in Europe and America, bringing a message of love, harmony and beauty that was both the quintessence of Sufi teaching and a revolutionary new approach to the harmonizing of Western and Eastern spirituality. He established a school of spiritual training based upon traditional Sufi teachings infused with the vision of the unity of religious ideals and the awakening of humanity to the divinity within. Inayat Khan died in India in 1927, leaving a significant body of recorded discourse and instruction on all things pertaining to spiritual ideals in the midst of life in the world.

For more information on Sufism
and the heritage of Hazrat Inayat Khan
contact:

Sufi Order International Secretariat of North America
P.O. Box 480
New Lebanon, NY 12125

www.sufiorder.org